MASTER YOUR SUPERPOWERS

AN INVALUABLE RESOURCE FOR CREATING A HAPPY LIFE

ALICE INOUE

DEDICATION

To my readers, who inspire me to write every day.

SPECIAL ACKNOWLEDGMENT

Alan

You continue to inspire me with your wisdom, dedication, authenticity, and guidance. I credit you with where I am today. You've influenced my path in life profoundly, and I am deeply grateful for the life we share.

ACKNOWLEDGMENTS

Jason Suapaia – How incredible it is that we have had the opportunity to collaborate. I cherish your insights, your talent, and your out-of-this-world ability to spark ideas within me. Your brain is beyond inspiring and your illustrative powers are divine. I'm extremely grateful that you were a part of this book and could bring my Superheroes to life. May you continue to trust yourself and open up to a world of possibilities you never knew existed.

Sarah Aschenbach – Here we are in year ten, working on book eight together! The way you edit my words to perfection continues to inspire and amaze me. The way the universe brought us together continues to spark joy within me. May your life continue to blossom in ways that light up your heart.

Dr. John Demartini - Your presence in my life over the last ten years has had the greatest impact on my growth and led me to my greatest clarity. Because of you, I'm actively fulfilling my purpose in life.

Dr. Ray Oshiro - Your time, wisdom, enthusiasm, and willingness to take me on as a student has inspired me to the next level. I am grateful and appreciative of you.

Tracy Wright Corvo - Thank you for your friendship and for your incredible photographic talent through the years.

SPECIAL THANKS

Happiness U Members, Teachers, Scholarship Students, and Supporters – Erin Ushijima, Kristin Lobdell, Jacque Vaughn, Shari Kimoto, David Marks, Chad Sato, Valerie Moriwaki, Yancey Unequivocally, Cory Jim, Jason Lent, Ron Nagasawa, Todd Nacapuy, Judy Segawa, Karen Murashige, Dave Miyamoto, Nancy Wong, Joyce Timpson, Shelley Morisaki, Kurt Osaki, Nocturna, Kristin Herrick, Helen Lee, Randi Miyagi, Jett Arii, Marie-Jose Noyle, Christian Bessee, Kimi Morton, Pua Pakele & Cabot, Mi Kosasa, Susan Toyama, Tanna and Bryson Dang, Laine Kohama, William Findley, Patti Hokama, Keoni Vaughn, Karen Nakaoka, E-Jay Maldonado, Alison Hayashi, Leanne Ferrer, Malia Johnson, Mae Luzod, Dr. Sheri Slogett. And of course, my business coach, Anastacia Brice. You are each incredibly important and special to me.

Clients, Friends, and Family – You have enriched my life so fully and helped me in infinite ways throughout the years. And, to my mother and my brother— thank you! I am who I am because of you.

TABLE OF CONTENTS

INTRODUCTION

The purpose of this book is to help you live your life to your best potential by understanding and developing your unique superpowers in a fun, yet significant way. You came into this life as a powerful human being, fully equipped with everything you need to master life, but you may have gotten sidetracked or knocked down by life's challenges.

If you've forgotten how to access your powers, feel a bit weak in life mastery, or simply need to gain confidence in yourself and life once again, I'd love for this book to be your guide. The ability to find the strength of who you are and remain positive in every situation that comes along is something we can get good at if we know ourselves and our best life strategy. The more we can live in our authentic power, the better we can handle anything that comes our way.

For ease of use, I've divided the book into four parts. In Part One, I share the ancient five-element system of Water, Wood, Fire, Earth, and Metal that is commonly used in eastern philosophy and energy disciplines. These five elements are symbolically represented within our personalities in varying degrees.

To identify your strongest elements, I've created a simple quiz for you to take. The results from the quiz will reveal your top two dominant elements (out of five) and will relate them to two superhero archetypes you will most closely identify with. I've personified these elements and presented them symbolically in the form of archetypal superheroes.

In Part Two, you will discover your own personal *Integrated Archetype* (IA), which is a blend of your primary and secondary elements. Every IA has a section devoted to it and offers an abundance of insight and guidance specific for that archetype. You'll also be able to better understand your IA self as well as your compatibility with others. There are twenty Integrated Archetypes in total.

Part Three is an organized list of the most common weaknesses characteristic to your Integrated Archetype. Everything from anger and fear to negative self-talk and procrastination is addressed, and simple direction and guidance for each are offered to help you to overcome or at least neutralize them so they don't hold you back in this journey of life.

Part Four places focus on the superpowers we all have as human beings, as well as the superweapons we can use to get through life more easily. This information will make a big contribution to allowing you to experience life in a positive and empowering way, no matter what challenges you may encounter. From appreciation and gratitude to visualization and manifestation, everything you need to be your most powerful self is here.

I believe that every one of us has universal "superpowers" within us that are unique to who we are, just waiting to be tapped into, developed, and fully utilized. This book is a fun way to identify with your superpowers, increase your arsenal of positive life "superweapons" and get direction on how to master them so you can transcend your personal life challenges.

Ultimately, we are most inspired when we know how to use our own, unique superpowers to help others move through their lives in a more positive and joyful way. May this book guide you towards your most powerful self!

PART ONE

LIFE, ELEMENTS, AND SUPERHERO ARCHETYPES

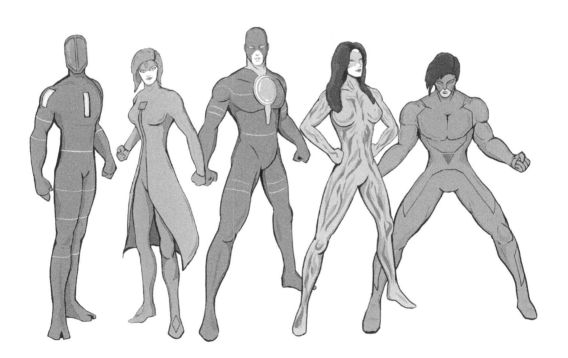

CHAPTER 1

The Journey of Life

I believe you were born for a reason and that you have a destiny and a path that is unique to your purpose. I also believe that there is an infinitely bigger picture to your life that you might not be completely aware of at times. Therefore, sometimes what you must endure and why things happen the way they do don't seem to make sense.

Have you ever looked back on your life and seen how perfectly certain happenings are connected? I'm sure you have, and that you've also seen how a past challenge catalyzed something within you that is now serving you in a powerful way. Often, it's after we make it through our challenges that we realize what we are capable of. However, while we are dealing with the challenge, we sometimes feel that we are not as strong as we'd like to be.

One thing I love about life is the freedom we have. We can choose to see things differently, to take different actions than in the past, and to prepare for life's inevitable trials by tapping into our greatest source of power – our Self. The more we know ourselves and trust ourselves, the more potential, power, and wisdom we have to draw upon when we are stressed by life.

Why is life difficult? If everything were easy, you would have no reason to be here. You are here to evolve and grow through the experiences of your life, and what's most important in this journey of life is how you experience your life every day.

The Journey of You

It might feel strange to think about this, but you are the only person you will be with for the rest of your life, and when all is said and done, you are the only one who will ultimately experience all that you are. As important as we are to ourselves, our lives revolve around a series of relationships from the moment we arrive on this planet to the moment we depart.

While it's true you wouldn't know yourself if you didn't spend time with others, it's interesting that, with all the time we spend time cultivating friendships, we are not normally taught to spend time cultivating the most important relationship of all – the one we have with ourselves.

Who Are You?

Do you really know who you are? At some point when you were a child, you knew what it was like to be yourself, and there was power in this knowing. You had unencumbered ideas and dreamed-of possibilities. You might have even fancied yourself to be Wonder Woman or Superman and had plans to use your powers to conquer the world. What's important about this is that you believed that you had power and that you could do certain things because no one had yet told you that you couldn't.

Our Need for Power

Power is an essential component of life. When we have it, we are effective and are able to influence. People with money, in the media, or in other leadership roles are thought of as people who have power. When we own it, we are confident that we can make things happen.

While not all of us have power in the form of money or status, we all have a form of power called *authentic power.* Authentic power is a specific type of power that is within us. Authentic power is not about commanding and controlling an outcome, but rather about the power that arises from within us as we evolve. We can cultivate this power by getting to know ourselves better. The stronger our authentic power is, the easier it is to transcend life's challenges as they come along.

Your Authentic Power

When we live in our authentic power, we are confident and more easily able to overcome fear, face challenges, and be free from inhibition. It's about being tuned in to who we are at our core so that we move through life in the direction that we desire.

Once we start to own who we are and live in our authentic power, we still must constantly work on maintaining it, because living in our authentic power is an ongoing process. Just as life brings us new challenges, we need to continue bringing our personal power to the plate.

What Living in Your Authentic Power Looks Like?

Living in your authentic power means that you commit to what you want and trust that you can handle anything that comes your way. It means that you are able to live in the present moment without too much worry about the past or the future.

Living a fulfilling and authentically powerful life involves knowing your purpose, understanding and accepting yourself as you are, and living your life in a way that inspires you. When your highest priority becomes working on *you*, the magic of supercharging your authentic power begins!

CHAPTER 2
Elements and Archetypes

The Five Elements

One way to explore in depth who we are is to use the five-element system from China. It's an ancient system used in Asian healing practices such as acupuncture and in disciplines such as feng shui. It is based on the theory that the world we live in is composed of the elements of Water, Wood, Fire, Earth, and Metal, and that these same elemental forces also exist symbolically within all human beings.

By looking at our personality and temperament through the elemental system, we can better understand our own distinct patterns of behavior and get deeper insight into our motivations and those of others.

This book uses the five elements as the framework upon which the superhero archetypes (who you'll be introduced to next) are developed. It's a fun and simple, yet deeply enlightening way to get confirmation and useful direction on how to stay balanced so as to further our authentic power on all levels - physically, mentally, emotionally, and spiritually.

Archetypes

Archetypes are common behavioral patterns that we share with everyone human, regardless of culture, status, gender, or age. As human beings, we make more sense of our own lives when we are able to identify with what we have in common with others.

Every day, we unconsciously live by the many archetypal patterns we have within us, as they embody core elements of what makes us who we are. These archetypal patterns have their own set of values, desires, powers, fears, strengths, weaknesses, personality traits, and more.

Archetypes answer these two questions: "Who am I?" and "Who are we?" They give us the power to see ourselves as individuals, yet also show us how we are connected collectively. Archetypes are like a shortcut to seeing your unwritten rules and unconscious behaviors in a new way.

In this book I've personified each one of the five elements and brought them all to life by transforming them into five superhero archetypes. Each superhero represents one of the five elements. Being aware of the strongest archetypal elemental patterns within you will not only affirm and inform who you are, but also empower you to be your best and most powerful self!

What's Your Elemental Superhero?

What are your top elemental superhero archetypes? Take the quiz in the next section to identify yours. When you read the superhero archetypes that you scored highest on, you'll notice that they will resonate deeply with you. You will see a reflection of yourself in them - and hopefully find this exciting!

Superhero Archetype Quiz

Using the following scale of 1-5, with 1 being nothing like you and 5 being exactly like you, answer according to how you feel inside and where you are in your life *now*, not how you think you should feel or be or how you were in the past. If you come across a question for which you relate to both descriptions equally, don't overthink it, go with your initial gut response.

5 Yes! Exactly like me.

4 Yes. Quite like me.

3 On the fence/not sure.

2 No. Not really like me.

1 No! Definitely nothing like me.

SUPERHERO ARCHETYPE ONE

_____ I think of myself as introspective and a deep thinker.

_____ I tend to go with the flow when plans change.

_____ I am quiet when first meeting people until I feel comfortable.

_____ I tend to dislike superficial people or conversations.

_____ I consider myself creative and imaginative.

_____ I prefer to stay out of the spotlight and work behind the scenes.

_____ I deal with insecurity, although others may not know it.

_____ I tend to be the one to over-give in relationships.

_____ I have a strong desire and need for intimacy and closeness.

_____ I am sensitive to criticism, negativity, harshness, and extremes.

_____ I prefer not to argue and dislike conflict.

_____ I prefer to stay home and cozy up rather than dress up for a party.

_____ I am quite private and share my feelings with a trusted few.

_____ I prefer having a few close friends over a large group of friends.

_____ I can get caught in nostalgia and dwell on the past.

_____ Total: **SUPERHERO ARCHETYPE ONE**

SUPERHERO ARCHETYPE TWO

_____ I am active and achievement-oriented.

_____ I pursue hobbies and activities that tend to be a bit competitive.

_____ I do not like to deal with authority figures.

_____ I get irritated when others are slow and waste my time.

_____ I become restless and impatient when I am stressed.

_____ I care about people but don't worry a lot about hurting their feelings.

_____ I need to do things my own way, and I have strong opinions.

_____ I have no trouble setting personal boundaries with others.

_____ I am not a fan of compromise but will do so if needed to keep the peace.

_____ I seem to be always doing something, even when at home.

_____ I have a lot of projects going on at once.

_____ I communicate well through either the spoken or written word.

_____ I am very curious and ask a lot of questions.

_____ I can be sarcastic and witty all at once.

_____ I can be quite judgmental and critical of others.

_____ **Total: SUPERHERO ARCHETYPE TWO**

SUPERHERO ARCHETYPE THREE

_____ I am fun to be around, or so I am told.

_____ I love to entertain or be entertained by others.

_____ I am always on the go and like to keep moving.

_____ I have a deeper than average aversion to pain.

_____ I am quite popular and invited to many events, gatherings, and parties.

_____ I love attention and have no problem being in the spotlight.

_____ I can get up and speak in front of people quite easily.

_____ I tend to be impulsive and spontaneous and bored by the dull and routine.

_____ I tend to be optimistic and enthusiastic about life, or so others say.

_____ I rarely turn down an opportunity to socialize.

_____ I am generous to a fault. Even if I'm low on resources, I'll offer to treat.

_____ I get bored with slow events and people who move slowly.

_____ I get distracted by fun and pleasure and choose it over getting work done.

_____ I love receiving gifts and being the recipient of attention.

_____ I like living in the moment and celebrating the moment.

_____ **Total: SUPERHERO ARCHETYPE THREE**

SUPERHERO ARCHETYPE FOUR

_____ I enjoy nurturing, caring for others, and creating comfort.

_____ I consider myself there for my friends and happy to help out.

_____ It takes me a while to get started when I have no immediate deadline.

_____ I'm thorough and often others need to wait for me to start or finish.

_____ I am seen as the peacemaker of the family.

_____ I am conservative in my thinking as well as when it comes to risk-taking.

_____ I prefer to wear cozy, comfortable clothing whenever I can.

_____ I tend to put others' needs before my own.

_____ I resist change even when I know it's needed.

_____ I realize it's easy for me to get stuck in a rut, even though I need routine.

_____ I feel guilty if I say no when someone asks me for help.

_____ I am indecisive and get overwhelmed in stressful situations.

_____ I'm fair and diplomatic and tend to see both sides of most situations.

_____ I feel the need to apologize for things that are not my fault.

_____ I am not competitive.

_____ **Total: SUPERHERO ARCHETYPE FOUR**

SUPERHERO ARCHETYPE FIVE

_____ It's important to me to be on time for appointments.

_____ I tend to over-analyze things, especially when they're important to me.

_____ I worry about things not going perfectly. I like things to go as planned.

_____ I have very high standards for myself as well as others.

_____ I am considered picky about things when I travel or eat out.

_____ I need to be in control, and that can drive my friends and family crazy.

_____ I have trouble when schedules and plans change at the last minute.

_____ I have rituals and processes that I use, and I stick by them whenever I can.

_____ I do not like to show strong emotions.

_____ I tend to judge others harshly and can be unforgiving when wronged.

_____ I dislike carelessness in others. If they do something, they should do it right.

_____ I can work patiently, slowly, and methodically until my tasks are finished.

_____ I have a hard time having fun when I am under stress.

_____ I avoid conflict whenever I can.

_____ I work well alone or one-on-one, not in customer service type jobs.

_____ **Total: SUPERHERO ARCHETYPE FIVE**

Your Score

Each archetype has a minimum low score of 15 and a maximum high score of 75. Add up your scores for each segment of the test, and write them below. The elemental correlation for each superhero is shown.

_____SUPERHERO ONE: **Water**

_____SUPERHERO TWO: **Wood**

_____SUPERHERO THREE: **Fire**

_____SUPERHERO FOUR: **Earth**

_____SUPERHERO FIVE: **Metal**

List your archetypes in score order, from highest to lowest. The two superhero archetypes with the highest score are your *dominant elemental qualities*. The archetype you scored highest on is your *primary* archetype, and your second-highest score is your *secondary* archetype. The element with the lowest score indicates the energy that is least present in your life.

If any of your top archetype scores are tied, read the two corresponding Integrated Archetype descriptions to see which one you resonate with the most.

Remember, there is no "good" or "bad" archetype, and one elemental emphasis is no better than another. Each archetype has its own positive and negative attributes.

Once you have clarified the two types you score highest in, turn to the next chapter to read about the Elemental Superhero Archetypes you are matched with.

CHAPTER 3

Meet the Elemental Superheroes

The elemental superhero archetypes collectively represent a combination of forces that we all have within us, but the two (or maybe three) that you scored highest on is what is you express most dominantly. As you read the profiles, see how you relate to the superhero archetypes that you scored highest on. Note how you feel when you read the profile of your lowest element. You will likely not relate at all.

The elements also come into play in your relationships. For example, you will most naturally resonate with people who have the same dominant elements as yours, or people whose elements are "supportive" in relation to you. Those who have a "controlling" element in relation to you will be more challenging for you, but also potentially more enriching if you use their influence to evolve and develop.

How the Elements Relate to Each Other

To understand how this works in your relationships, it helps to understand how the five elements are connected in nature. They work together in two very amazing ways—either supporting or controlling.

The *supportive cycle* (also known as the *creative cycle* or the *generative cycle*) places the elements in a circle in a specific order. Each element supports and leads to another in the same way that day turns into night or one season turns into another.

This is how the elements line up to *support* each other:
- Water nourishes Wood (trees and plants need Water to grow)
- Wood feeds Fire (the fuel for Fire is Wood)
- Fire creates Earth (ashes from a Fire replenish Earth)
- Earth births Metal (gold and ore are mined from the Earth)
- Metal transforms to Water (when Metal is heated, it changes to liquid)

The *controlling cycle* (also known as the *destructive cycle* or the *transformative cycle*) shows how the elements cyclically consume each other versus how they support each other.

This is how the elements line up to *control* each other:

- Water puts out Fire (Fire is extinguished by Water)
- Fire melts Metal (Metal is burned by Fire)
- Metal chops Wood (Wood can be cut with an axe)
- Wood depletes Earth (Earth is penetrated by growing trees)
- Earth dams Water (Water is absorbed by Earth)

The supportive and controlling cycles clearly show how natural forces interact. When the elements are in equilibrium, you sense more peace and harmony. When they are in conflict or out of balance, you may experience more obstacles. It's the same in our relationships.

How Your Elemental Archetype Relates to Other Archetypes

As an example, if your dominant elemental archetype is Fire and your partner is Wood, because "Wood feeds Fire" in the supportive cycle, the two of you for the most part are likely to get along great. Your partner has the ideas and creativity that supports your desire to take action and go out and get things done.

If, however, your partner is a strong Water, you would gravitate towards staying home and being more private, even though the Fire in you would tend toward socializing and interacting with others.

If your two top elements are Fire and Water, you would see the traits of both within you.

Profile Insights

Every elemental superhero has a name, gender, superpower, virtue, weakness, motto, core desire, and fear, along with many other attributes. The key to remember as you are reading through them, is that the specifics may not match exactly, but likely there will be enough that you will find resonance.

Also, while the superheroes are depicted as male or female, this simply refers to masculine or feminine aspects of personality expression. In other words, a male person may have the female archetypes of Earth (Talitha) and Water (Selene) as his highest scores. This simply means that his personality expression has those qualities. Remember, we all have masculine and feminine expression within us to varying degrees.

THE ELEMENTAL SUPERHEROES

SELENE

Superhero Archetype One: Water

This archetype succeeds in overcoming life's challenges by trusting her intuition. Her deep connection with the unseen and the ability to let go and sink into the depths of life's flow, help her to conquer her fear and master life at all levels. Her creativity allows her to conjure up visions of possibility that flow towards manifestation when she is in balance. When unbalanced, fear takes over, emotions spin out of control, and only time and isolation can restore her balance.

Gender	Female
Element	Water
Superpower	Intuition
Virtue	Connection
Deficiency of Virtue	Fear
Excess of Virtue	Over emotional
Other Superpowers	Vision, Creativity, Tenacity, Persuasion
Weaknesses	Moody, insecure, manipulative, detached, dependent, hypersensitive, clingy
Life Difficulties	Creating a life that is balanced physically, mentally, emotionally, and spiritually; taking downtime without feeling guilty
When Stressed	Internalizes, isolates, lets fear make decisions
Motto	"I care."
Core Desires	To be needed; to protect, help, and care for others
Core Value	To feel love
Life Goals	Nurturing and growing people and ideas; discovering meaning and purpose
Basic Fears	Being thought of as selfish; losing security
Life Strategies	Helping others; using ritual and symbolism to make sense of life
Habits to Break	Over-giving; holding on long after it's time to let go; addiction to comfort even when change is needed
Personality Traits	Introverted, flowing, adaptable, pliant
Shape	Undefined, wavy
Power Colors	Black, Charcoal, Navy-Blue
Power Number	2
Planet Affiliation	Moon
Season Affiliation	Winter
Hour Affiliation	Dusk
Yin-Yang Phase	Full Yin
Energy Pattern	Conservative
Mythological Alliance	Mermaid
Animal Affiliation	Dolphin, Turtle
Also known as	Philosopher, Entrepreneur, Guide, Innovator, Mystic

NEXUS

Superhero Archetype Two: Wood

This archetype succeeds in overcoming life's challenges by being adaptable. Their ability to quickly tap into their resources of intelligence and determination gets them past obstacles, no matter how challenging. They always come out ahead. Their ability to make progress is what takes them to new levels of achievement throughout life. When unbalanced, they become anxious and indecisive and start blaming and complaining. It's only when they can tap into their large well of creativity that they can create a new reality, allowing them to move forward once again.

Gender	Androgynous
Element	Wood
Superpower	Adaptability
Virtue	Creativity
Deficiency of Virtue	Indecision
Excess of Virtue	Anxiety
Other Superpowers	Intelligence, Determination, Logic, Resources
Weaknesses	Gossipy, wasting time, quick to anger, impatient, blunt
Life Difficulties	Slowing down; feeling compassion for others
When Stressed	Blames, complains, loses focus
Motto	"I can make it happen."
Core Desires	To be uniquely myself
Core Value	To make progress; to be efficient
Life Goals	To organize the world; to turn ideas into action
Basic Fears	Being bored; not knowing enough; not getting ahead
Life Strategies	To take action; to enjoy life and all its experiences
Habits to Break	Always feeling the need to do something
Personality Traits	Extroverted, striving, controlling, flexible, self-assured
Shape	Columnar
Power Colors	Greens, Blues
Power Number	5
Planet Affiliation	Mercury
Season Affiliation	Spring
Hour Affiliation	Dawn
Yin-Yang Phase	New Yang
Energy Pattern	Expansive
Mythological Alliance	Pegasus
Animal Affiliation	Eagle, Butterfly
Also known as	Trailblazer, Mover and Shaker, Pioneer, Visionary, Professional

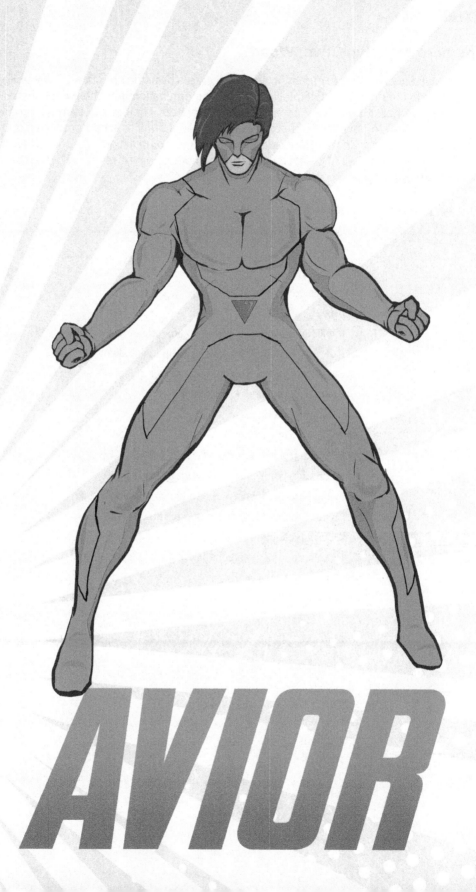

AVIOR

AVIOR

Superhero Archetype Three: Fire

This archetype succeeds in overcoming life's challenges by being positive, no matter the obstacle or challenge. His ability to be confident in life and his belief that no matter what, things are going to be okay, is what allows him to shine brightly, even on the darkest of days. When unbalanced, ego and impatience take over, causing him to make choices that produce panic and anxiety. Only when he can shine light on his darkest fears can he once again rise to the pinnacle of optimism and bring back the spotlight of hope.

Gender	Male
Element	Fire
Superpower	Positivity
Virtue	Confidence
Deficiency of Virtue	Negativity
Excess of Virtue	Arrogance
Other Superpowers	Enthusiasm, Courage, Optimism, Self-motivation
Weaknesses	Stubborn; greedy; impulsive; impatient; egotistical
Life Difficulties	Focusing on others' needs; always needing attention
When Stressed	Becomes anxious, panics
Motto	"Now that I'm here, the party can start."
Core Desires	To be worthy, be truly happy, to have fun experiences
Core Value	To be loyal
Life Goals	To be happy; to get to paradise; to improve the world
Basic Fears	Being shut out or unloved; being admonished for being wrong
Life Strategies	Being as strong as possible; winning; being present and enjoying every moment
Habits to Break	Overexertion
Personality Traits	Extroverted, dynamic, sparkling, enthusiastic
Shape	Triangular
Power Colors	Red, Purple, Orange
Power Number	1
Planet Affiliation	Sun
Season Affiliation	Summer
Hour Affiliation	Noon
Yin-Yang Phase	Full Yang
Energy Pattern	Completive
Mythological Alliance	Dragon
Animal Affiliation	Lion, Horse
Also known as	Partner, Friend, Warrior, Winner, Performer, Creator, Storyteller

TALITHA

Superhero Archetype Four: Earth

This archetype succeeds in overcoming life's challenges by being patient. She knows that by not rushing the outcome and taking into consideration all aspects of the spectrum of challenges, a good outcome will manifest in time. Her ability to stay calm and patient allows her to effortlessly draw to her circumstances that help her form a solid foundation for the next phase. When unbalanced, she loses her center, becomes dependent on others, and worries excessively about outcomes. Only when she can see her value can she bring herself back to stability.

Gender	Female
Element	Earth
Superpower	Patience
Virtue	Consideration
Deficiency of Virtue	Submissiveness
Excess of Virtue	Entitlement
Other Superpowers	Decisiveness, Calm, Perseverance, Benevolence, Practicality
Weaknesses	Bending to please; deriving self-value from others; dependence; stubbornness; procrastination
Life Difficulties	Resistance to change; speaking up
When Stressed	Worries excessively and feels hopeless; holds onto things
Motto	"We are all equal." "I always lend a helping hand."
Core Desires	To connect with others; to please others
Core Value	To belong, to keep the peace
Life Goals	To be real; to be authentic
Basic Fears	Being alone; feeling unwanted
Life Strategies	Being one of the gang; being down-to-earth; making people feel better
Habits to Break	Losing oneself to please others; over-apologizing; holding resentment
Personality Traits	Introverted, solid, stable, reliable, grounded, sweet
Shape	Square
Power Colors	Yellow, Gold, Sand, Brown
Power Number	6
Planet Affiliation	Venus
Season Affiliation	Late Summer
Hour Affiliation	Sunset
Yin-Yang Phase	Full Yin
Energy Pattern	Conservative
Mythological Alliance	Leprechaun
Animal Affiliation	Bull, Dog
Also known as	The Stable One, Nurturer, Listener, Supporter

ALCOR

Superhero Archetype Five: Metal

This archetype succeeds in overcoming life's challenges by his ability to focus. His clarity, mental acuity, and desire for perfection allow him to expertly slice through obstacles to get to the next level. He knows that, no matter what, if he doesn't give up, he will be successful in his power. When imbalanced, he either overanalyzes and gets stuck, or he ends up charging forward impatiently before he is ready. Only when he can connect to his ability to control the moment can he bring back his power.

Gender	Male
Element	Metal
Superpower	Focus
Virtue	Commitment
Deficiency of Virtue	Impatience
Excess of Virtue	Reactivity
Other Superpowers	Responsibility, Strong Leadership, Perfectionism, Clear-headedness
Weaknesses	Picky, judgmental, being a know-it-all, inability to share emotions
Life Difficulties	Searching for a perfection that doesn't exist
When Stressed	Cold, emotionless, detached, aloof
Motto	"Structure and schedules run the world." "Information is more important than entertainment."
Core Desires	To finish, to complete
Core Value	To be organized; to be graceful
Life Goals	To stay in control
Basic Fears	Losing control; feeling unable to achieve desires; getting stuck in emotions
Life Strategies	Being one with change
Habits to Break	Analysis-paralysis; locking into a line of thinking; not being open
Personality Traits	Introverted, organized, strong, durable, cool
Shape	Circle
Power Colors	Silver, Pastels, White
Power Number	9
Planet Affiliation	Mars
Season Affiliation	Autumn
Hour Affiliation	Midnight
Yin-Yang Phase	New Yin
Energy Pattern	Contractive
Mythological Alliance	Sphinx, Unicorn
Animal Affiliation	Cat, Panther
Also known as	Professional, Judge, Scholar, Geek, King, Alchemist

PART TWO

INTEGRATED SUPERHERO ARCHETYPES

PRIMARY ▶ / SECONDARY ▼	WATER	WOOD
WATER		WOOD - WATER **LOGICAL VISIONARY**
WOOD	WATER - WOOD **RESOURCEFUL CREATOR**	
FIRE	WATER - FIRE **INTUITIVE LUMINARY**	WOOD - FIRE **INNOVATIVE IDEALIS**
EARTH	WATER - EARTH **REFLECTIVE CONFIDANT**	WOOD - EARTH **THRIVING MANIFESTOR**
METAL	WATER - METAL **CARING PERFECTIONIST**	WOOD - METAL **FLEXIBLE RULE-MAKER**

FIRE	EARTH	METAL

FIRE - WATER
RADIANT PROVIDER

EARTH - WATER
CALM CONNECTOR

METAL - WATER
FOCUSED VISIONARY

FIRE - WOOD
SPONTANEOUS INITIATOR

EARTH - WOOD
PATIENT SPEEDSTER

METAL - WOOD
EFFICIENT PRODUCER

EARTH - FIRE
LOYAL CHEERLEADER

METAL - FIRE
DEDICATED ENTHUSIAST

FIRE - EARTH
ENERGETIC PROTECTOR

METAL - EARTH
MASTERFUL ALLY

FIRE - METAL
WARM-HEARTED LONER

EARTH - METAL
RELIABLE ANALYST

CHAPTER 4
The Integrated Archetypes

Your Integrated Archetype Is Important

Discovering your Integrated Archetype is like finding your personality's innate superpower. This knowledge adds value to your life and to your ability to stay in balance, which will help you transcend life's challenges.

Your Integrated Archetype reveals how you intentionally or unintentionally express yourself and the way you most naturally are. You might have wondered why at times you are shy and introverted, and at other times bold and extroverted. Or why, in some areas of life, you are logical and linear while in others you are creative and out-of-the-box. This can be explained through knowledge of the particular elemental combination that makes up your Integrated Archetype.

The explanations will give you greater perspective on what you need to achieve balance. It will also help you understand others around you and how they fit into your life. The purpose is to aid you in finding power within yourself and creating harmony in your interactions.

Below, you'll find a list of your superpowers, energy-balancing activities, your creed and purpose, where your support comes from, who your greatest teachers are, and more. When you focus on strengthening your positives, your superpowers shine, and you'll be able to serve your sphere of influence in a much more meaningful and dynamic way.

INTEGRATED ARCHETYPE GLOSSARY

The various categories of the twenty Integrated Archetypes are defined here for your reference as needed.

PRIMARY ELEMENT: The element with the highest score on your test.

SECONDARY ELEMENT: The element with the second highest score on your test.

OVERVIEW: This is a general description of your Integrated Archetype.

YOUR PURPOSE: This is your Integrated Archetype's primary purpose.

YOUR CREED: A creed is a belief that drives your thoughts and behaviors. Your personal creed must be one that you believe in, but it doesn't have to be accepted by others. There's no right and wrong to your creed. The word credo comes from Latin and means "I believe." You cannot do what you say if you don't know what you believe. The creed that is listed is a prompt for you to consider what you actually believe in. *Please change or rewrite the one given to best suit you.*

AT YOUR BEST: This is a description of how you naturally operate when you are in balance physically, mentally, emotionally, and spiritually. If you don't see any of these qualities within yourself now, know that they do exist and are just dormant within you currently. Once you achieve balance, these traits will emerge organically.

AT YOUR WORST: If you see that you don't demonstrate any of these behaviors in your expression of self, that is great! You are likely operating in a very balanced way and may have transcended these traits from the past. Or, you may find that they show up only when you are stressed and overwhelmed. The key is to know that when you do exhibit or feel these emotions arising, it's wise to slow down and pay attention to yourself and your own needs to restore balance and live your purpose.

YOUR ARCHETYPE TWIN: This is your "mirror" archetype. It has exactly the same two top elements as yours, but its primary element is your secondary element and vice-versa. For example, if you are a Water + Fire, your archetype twin is Fire + Water.

What does this mean? The twin is the archetype that most closely resembles you. Fundamentally, it mirrors you, but with subtle differences. Under different circumstances or in different moods, your archetypes could almost change places. And if you have an archetype twin in your life, you feel a natural connection. This is someone who "gets" you, and you them. You might notice that when you are together, you operate with the same dynamic. You match each other in ways that are inspiring and you get along easily. The traits that you love in yourself are the traits that you love in them, and vice-versa.

The challenge comes when one of you is out of balance, stressed, or having a bad day and not operating optimally. It is then that you may experience some irritation, as the twin's purpose in your life is to bring to your awareness your disowned parts—the parts of you that you don't want to think you have even though you actually do; you just haven't accepted yet.

Since one of the purposes of life is to grow in self-awareness, at times your archetype twin's purpose in your life is to do just that—teach you to accept and love yourself as you are.

MOST COMPATIBLE WITH: These are people you get along with almost effortlessly. At times you're there for them, and at other times, they are there for you. These are people you feel very "at home" with. The relationship flows naturally and with ease. This is because the mutual exchange of elements generates an even exchange of energy.

MOST SUPPORTED BY: These are people who are always there for you. It's not that you aren't there for them, but somehow, they just feel like the solid ground beneath your life, however you interact with them. You feel their support and trust their sincerity.

In these relationships, both elements that compose the other's Integrated Archetype "give" of themselves to your elements. It's wise to be especially appreciative of these people; let them know how important they are to you and how thankful you are to have them in your life.

MOST DRAINING FOR YOU: These are the people you feel you can spend only a limited amount of time with before you get tired. It's not that you don't like them or don't enjoy being with them; this combination of elements just operates on a different level, and being with them requires more of your energy and other resources. This is especially true when they do not feel empowered or when they are undergoing hardships and emotional challenges.

YOUR GREATEST TEACHER: Someone who is significant in your life for one of two reasons: either you have great respect for them and easily and willingly learn from their influence, or they are the most challenging people you have to deal with. Either way, they offer you the most growth. These relationships work best when you embrace these people as teachers, knowing that because of them you are more patient and understanding—a more evolved you. The elements of your greatest teachers are the two that directly challenge your elements.

YOUR ELEMENTAL DYNAMIC: All elements have a cyclical relationship to each other. They are designated as either "nurturing" or "controlling," depending on their phase of interaction with each other. Out of the twenty Integrated Archetypes, there are ten "nurturing" interactions and ten "controlling" interactions. Your top two elements will fall into one of these two categories.

Controlling: This means that your two elements relate in a way that one wants to take control of the other.

Nurturing: This means that your two elements relate in a way where one is more nurturing and supportive of the other.

MISSING ELEMENT: Your missing element is detailed here if your elemental dynamic is "controlling."

SUPPORTING ELEMENT: Your supporting element is detailed here if your elemental dynamic is "nurturing."

YOUR SUPERPOWERS: Your four top superpowers are listed here, based on your Integrated Archetype. Continue to add to your awareness of them as you develop, notice, and affirm them in your daily actions.

YOUR MISSION FOR POWER: Your daily actions make a difference in how you encounter and transcend your challenges. Focus on these missions, which you can incorporate daily. They detail and emphasize what you are good at and how you make a difference in your sphere of influence.

WEAKNESSES TO STRENGTHEN: These are areas that you may have either transcended or are still working on. As human beings, we will always have our weaknesses, our downsides, but the more conscious we are about them and the more we work on balance, the less they show up. Refer to Appendix A at the end of this chapter for some ways to temper and overcome your weaknesses.

LIFE AFFIRMATION: The word *affirmation* means to make something firm in your mind. Affirmations are phrases that we can repeat inwardly to help us maintain balance and stay on course. To maximize your potential, continue to develop your own affirmations.

ENERGY-BALANCING ACTIVITIES: We all experience periods of time when we feel out of balance. When you notice you are not operating at your best or are not feeling quite like yourself, you can look here to identify what you need. Embrace one of the suggested passive or active activities to balance out your energy.

THE INTEGRATED ARCHETYPES

Water + Wood

The Resourceful Creator

Aka: The Perceptive Pioneer and The Introspective Innovator

PRIMARY ELEMENT: Water (Selene)

SECONDARY ELEMENT: Wood (Nexus)

YOUR OVERVIEW: As a Resourceful Creator, you have the innate ability to envision possibilities where others see none and to create value seemingly out of nothing. You excel at moving thorough limitations. Because of who you are, you effortlessly draw people into alignment with what you believe in. You bring an invaluable source of *it's possible* energy to any project and thrive when you are challenged to come up with ideas and produce with a plan. In any initial encounter, you are naturally reserved, yet once you feel secure, you take control and make things happen.

You love asking questions, learning, and teaching. Sharing wisdom inspires you. People are drawn to your strength as a Perceptive Pioneer as you intuitively follow ideas that challenge the status quo. As an Introspective Innovator, you take the time to contemplate possibilities and come up with new ways to do old things, inspiring much needed progress in any industry in which you participate.

YOUR PURPOSE: You are here to show people that there's no limit to what is possible to achieve.

YOUR CREED: "If I can envision it, I can produce it."

YOUR CORE DESIRE: To not overextend yourself, to be authentically who you are.

YOUR CORE VALUE: To make progress and be accepted.

AT YOUR BEST: You are creative, spontaneous, organized, open, and adaptable. You can dig deep into the unseen world of thought, intuition, and creativity and come up with ideas and manifestations that amaze all who stand witness.

AT YOUR WORST: You are stubborn, inflexible, detached, and non-responsive. You are defensive and insecure and will isolate yourself and hide.

YOUR ARCHETYPE TWIN: Wood + Water – Logical Visionary

MOST COMPATIBLE WITH:

Fire + Water – Radiant Provider
Water + Fire – Intuitive Luminary

MOST SUPPORTED BY:

Metal + Water – Focused Visionary
Water + Metal – Caring Perfectionist

MOST DRAINING FOR YOU:

Fire + Wood – Spontaneous Initiator
Wood + Fire – Innovative Idealist

YOUR GREATEST TEACHER:

Metal + Earth – Masterful Ally
Earth + Metal – Reliable Analyst

YOUR ELEMENTAL DYNAMIC: Nurturing

Water nourishes Wood, and together they work synergistically to stimulate growth. When you are in balance, you are creative, thriving, and energetic, and you make great progress on your goals. However, since Wood drains Water, it's important to take time to nurture both elements and not depend solely on Wood to be the energy generator and make all the progress.

In other words, if you are overly active with too much Wood energy (constantly on the go, striving for success, working on being efficient, and focusing on productivity) and do not get enough downtime, rest, and time for reflection, which Water needs, you suffer from burnout. If, however, you are too laid back and get out of active mode, you lack the stimulus you need to be successful in the way you envision.

SUPPORTING ELEMENT: Metal

Metal acts as a support to the elements of Water and Wood. In the elemental cycle, Metal can transform itself into liquid (Water), which in turn fuels Wood. The one element both Water and Wood have as a support is Metal, so when you feel at odds with yourself, tired, or out of balance, it can be extremely helpful to bring Metal energy into your day. This might be in the form of getting organized, writing out a To Do list, creating a system, clearing out clutter (both physical and digital), or getting various other affairs in order. The more order you create, the more balanced you'll be.

Having Metal elements in your environment is essential for support. Shiny metal objects, and wall art depicting circular patterns are beneficial for Water/Wood Integrated Archetypes, as well as pastels and the colors white and light grey.

Metal energy is about precision and grace and drawing strong boundaries, so it is helpful to spend time with individuals who have Metal as a component of their makeup (e.g., Alcor – Superhero Archetype Five).

YOUR PERSONAL VIRTUES:

Emotionally Intelligent: You are excellent at reading situations and understanding the dynamics of any relationship.

Sensory: You have an ability to sense when issues arise that need a swift reaction and can change course before others even realize the need.

Immersive: You channel your energy so fully into what you create that you are able to concentrate deeply when you are intrigued.

Productive: You are more resourceful than most and can manage more on your plate than most. You may have multiple things going on, but you accomplish many tasks and pursue interests in depth.

Progressive: You look ahead and inspire others to move forward. You like to come out ahead and can tweak things as you move towards success.

YOUR SUPERPOWERS:

Intuition, Connection, Adaptability, Creativity

WEAKNESSES TO STRENGTHEN:

Defensiveness, Insecurity, Worry, Indecisiveness

YOUR MISSION FOR POWER:

Give yourself the gift of time. Carve out enough time in your schedule to get things done. You thrive when you are able to measure your productivity by seeing progress.

Make sure you know your completion dates. You love being busy, but you also need to know when you will be finished so that your commitments don't drag on and on. With each completion, you gain energy.

Nurture the people and projects around you. It is in your nature to share your knowledge and help others grow. Remember that others may not develop as quickly as you expect them to. Be patient.

Take time to reflect and renew. Something inside you wants to keep going, but just as important as movement is rest. Make sure you cease all activity and let yourself "do nothing" from time to time, as this is when the ideas and inspiration flow.

Follow your feelings. Though you are logical and practical, your sense of intuition is extremely strong. For the most success in all you do, be open to letting your heart lead the way.

LIFE AFFIRMATION: "I am exactly where I need to be in my life."

Whenever you think you need to be further along, stop and ask who you are comparing yourself to. Comparisons do nothing but make you feel bad, and making yourself feel bad is not the path to success and happiness. If you are going to compare, be fair and loving—compare you to you. Look back at where you were and acknowledge the gains you've made. Look at what you have done and applaud your progress. Your success has nothing to do with anyone else. Everything is about you. You have the power to ruin your day or to make your day.

ENERGY-BALANCING ACTIVITIES: (Refer to Appendix A at the end of Part Two for ideas.)

When you feel emotional: Earth activities

When you feel mentally stressed: Metal activities

When you feel burnt-out: Water activities

When you feel stuck: Wood activities

When you feel uninspired: Fire activities

SELENE AVIOR

Water + Fire

The Intuitive Luminary

Aka: The Enigmatic Optimist and The Introverted Extrovert

PRIMARY ELEMENT: Water (Selene)

SECONDARY ELEMENT: Fire (Avior)

YOUR OVERVIEW: As an Intuitive Luminary, you innately understand what others need. You excel at inspiring others with ideas and can build vivid images of the positive impact that you believe in. You are a positive source of energy and thrive when you are "feeling good" about life and all that's happening. You have a warm, engaging personality, although it can take you some time to adjust in a new environment.

Helping others make new connections inspires you. You delight in linking people to people or people to products, and you know who or what to connect or recommend. As an Enigmatic Optimist, people are drawn to your positivity. As an Introverted Extrovert, you are private and reserved and love your alone time, and yet you light up when you feel confident and are called on to share anything you are interested in or that furthers your purpose.

YOUR PURPOSE: You are here to be an inspiration to humanity and a source of healing.

YOUR CREED: "I exist in a limitless Universe, and I can achieve anything."

YOUR CORE DESIRE: To be accepted and needed while living a happy life in which you are able to do what you want.

YOUR CORE VALUE: To be loyal to love and do what inspires you.

AT YOUR BEST: You are calm yet energetic, optimistic, and creative. You are positive even in the face of challenges and are able to go with the flow of life.

AT YOUR WORST: You are withdrawn, insecure, overly impulsive, selfish, and self-centered. You take offense easily.

YOUR ARCHETYPE TWIN: Fire + Water - Radiant Provider

MOST COMPATIBLE WITH:

Metal + Earth – Masterful Ally
Earth + Metal – Reliable Analyst

MOST SUPPORTED BY:

Metal + Wood – Efficient Producer
Wood + Metal – Flexible Rule Maker

MOST DRAINING FOR YOU:

Wood + Earth – Thriving Manifestor
Earth + Wood – Patient Speedster

YOUR GREATEST TEACHER:

Earth + Water – Calm Connector
Water + Earth – Reflective Confidant

YOUR ELEMENTAL DYNAMIC: Controlling

Fire and Water together create steam, so when you are in a balanced state, you are powerful and dynamic. However, since Fire also can be put out by Water, it's important to take time to nurture both elements and not overdo one or the other.

If you are excessively active, and if you do not get enough downtime and rejuvenation, which Water needs, you suffer from depletion and burnout. However, if you spend too much time alone, you lack the stimulus you need to be creative and inspired.

MISSING ELEMENT: Wood

Wood bridges the elements of Water and Fire. In the elemental cycle, Water nurtures Wood, which in turn fuels Fire. The only thing Water and Fire have in common is Wood, so when you feel at odds with yourself, tired, or out of balance, being in "Wood" energy, like nature, is extremely helpful.

Having plants (real or silk) in your environment is essential for support. Wall art depicting nature and all shades of the color green are considered beneficial for Water/Fire Integrated Archetypes.

Wood energy is about moving forward and being adaptable, so it can be helpful to spend time with people who have Wood as a component of their makeup (e.g., Nexus – Superhero Archetype Two).

YOUR PERSONAL VIRTUES:

Profound: You see beyond the obvious and rarely draw a conclusion from a superficial viewpoint. You seldom miss what others overlook.

Magnetic: You have the ability to bring out the positive in people and situations, and people are drawn to your positive outlook and spirit.

Subtly Persuasive: You are subtle, yet influential in your ability to be persuasive. You excel at "selling" products and ideas that you believe in without actually selling them.

Perceptive: Your intuition when combined with confidence is second to none. You are sensitive to others' needs and know exactly what to say to lift another's spirits.

Admired: You are respected for your knowledge and your ability to connect to people. You excel in many things and are well liked and respected.

YOUR SUPERPOWERS:
Connection, Intuition, Positivity, Confidence

WEAKNESSES TO STRENGTHEN:
Insecurity, Defensiveness, Arrogance, Vanity

YOUR MISSION FOR POWER:

Encourage people often. Make sure to show appreciation for others, and make it a point to be specific about what. You will build engagement and happiness.

Remember that your attitude is contagious. People in your life have likely come to see that you are a great support to them. You are enthusiastic and energetic when they are down or are afraid of making a change. Your attitude is what helps them continue on. Over time, people will start to look to you for your wisdom and inspiration.

Protect yourself and your gifts. Insulate yourself from the people who drain your energy or who whine, blame, and complain too much. Make it a point to position yourself in environments that support you the best.

Connect people daily. Though you are aware of the hierarchy, boundaries, and silos that divide people from each other, the Water element within you gives you the ability to flow across borders. You can use this to open people up to new ideas and to previously unseen opportunities.

Help others understand the bigger picture. You have the ability to see things in a way that can help others understand what's going on. Share what you see, and you'll help others feel more at ease.

LIFE AFFIRMATION: "I see my desired reality so strongly that I attract the perfect situations and circumstances into my path to support me."

The more time you spend envisioning what you want to manifest versus focusing on the fear of *not* getting what you want, the stronger your power. Science has now proved that we create our own reality. Knowing this, it makes more sense than ever for you to put focus on what you want. As an Intuitive Luminary, you will "magically" find yourself in the right places at exactly the right time. You can be, do, or have anything you want in your life; you just have to use the power of your Water to envision your desires, and then use the illumination of your Fire element to attract them.

ENERGY-BALANCING ACTIVITIES: (Refer to Appendix A at the end of Part Two for ideas.)

When you feel emotional: Earth activities

When you feel mentally stressed: Metal activities

When you feel burnt-out: Water activities

When you feel stuck: Wood activities

When you feel uninspired: Fire activities

SELENE TALITHA

Water + Earth

The Reflective Confidant

Aka: The Endearing Peacemaker and The Nurturing Ambassador

PRIMARY ELEMENT: Water (Selene)

SECONDARY ELEMENT: Earth (Talitha)

YOUR OVERVIEW: People gravitate toward your ability as a Reflective Confidant to make them feel at ease. You are patient and practical, yet able to move towards your goals and manifest results. You excel at listening and relating to others and rarely hesitate to jump in when help is needed. You hold the space of calmness for others when they are in transition and provide unconditional support. People naturally trust you. You have a wonderful way of making everyone in the room feel loved and cherished.

Building connections, experiencing love, and belonging inspire you. You delight in cooperation and collaboration and tend to be a giver when push comes to shove. You also move at your own pace (a bit slower than average.) As an Endearing Peacemaker, you keep the peace with family and friends. As a Nurturing Ambassador, you show a high level of loyalty to those close to you, and you instinctively put energy into nurturing and growing relationships.

YOUR PURPOSE: You are here to find your own path while helping others find theirs.

YOUR CREED: "Everyone is welcome. Everyone is important."

YOUR CORE DESIRE: To be accepted as you are and not have to bend over backwards to please others.

YOUR CORE VALUE: To live in peace with love and minimal conflict.

AT YOUR BEST: You are loyal, considerate, and caring, yet also persistent and tenacious. You are incredibly creative and have the stamina to bring projects to fruition. You are decisive and calm, go with the flow, and follow your intuition.

AT YOUR WORST: You are stubborn, emotional, defensive, and over-sensitive. You hold on to the past for fear of what the future brings. You are lazy. You procrastinate. You worry excessively and tend to either overeat or overdo. You say what you think people want to hear and don't stand up for yourself.

YOUR ARCHETYPE TWIN: Earth + Water – Calm Connector

MOST COMPATIBLE WITH:

Fire + Wood – Spontaneous Initiator
Wood + Fire – Innovative Idealist

MOST SUPPORTED BY:

Fire + Metal – Warm-Hearted Loner
Metal + Fire – Dedicated Enthusiast

MOST DRAINING FOR YOU:

Water + Metal – Caring Perfectionist
Metal + Water – Focused Visionary

YOUR GREATEST TEACHER:

Water + Fire – Intuitive Luminary
Fire + Water – Radiant Provider

YOUR ELEMENTAL DYNAMIC: Controlling

Earth and Water together create stability, so when you are in balance, you are poised and calm. However, since Earth can also slow the flow of Water, it's important to take time to nurture both elements and not overdo one or the other.

If Earth energy starts dominating, you feel stuck and unable to move forward in new and dynamic ways—you're stuck in a rut. If there is too much Water energy and not enough Earth, which Water needs to keep it from draining away, you lose your center and are not able to draw strong boundaries around your time and energy.

MISSING ELEMENT: Metal

Metal bridges the elements of Earth and Water. In the elemental cycle, Earth produces Metal, which in turn transforms into Water. The only thing Earth and Water have in common is Metal, so when you feel at odds with yourself, drained, stuck, or out of balance, bringing Metal energy into your day can be extremely helpful. This can be in the form of getting organized, writing out a to do list, creating a system, clearing out clutter—both physical and digital—or getting other affairs in order. The more order you create, the more balanced you will be.

Having Metal elements in your environment is essential for support. Shiny metal objects, wall art depicting circular patterns, as well as pastels and the colors white and light grey are considered beneficial for Water/Earth Integrated Archetypes.

Metal energy is about precision and grace and drawing strong boundaries, so make it a point of spending time with individuals who have Metal as a part of their makeup (e.g., Alcor – Superhero Archetype Five).

YOUR PERSONAL VIRTUES:

Empathetic: You are able to read people and understand where they are coming from, even if you have never met them before.

Intuitive: You are extremely intuitive and able to find common ground, and you strike up a conversation easily.

Nuanced: You are delicate in the way you approach people and situations, and able to read between the lines.

Benevolent: You genuinely care about people and those who are close to your heart. You come across as kind and caring, even in professional settings.

Agreeable: You have a harmonious personality and make everyone feel comfortable. You're well-liked, and you are the one who keeps the peace around you.

YOUR SUPERPOWERS:

Intuition, Connection, Patience, Consideration

WEAKNESSES TO STRENGTHEN:

Insecurity, Dependency, Inability to say no, Over-giving

YOUR MISSION FOR POWER:

Remember, not everyone understands "connection." Some people have more rational minds. Don't spend too much time trying to convince others about energy. Your sense of connection is intuitive.

Hone techniques for saying no. It's okay to make time for yourself and self-nurture the same way you nurture others. Practice ways to turn down events.

Listen, but don't get caught up. Learn how to listen and relate to others without losing your energy. Remember, each of us is responsible for her own life, and it's not up to you to help everyone.

Represent others' voices. Although you don't naturally like to speak up for yourself, you have the ability to speak for others. Consider roles where you take responsibility for representing those who can't speak up for themselves. This would be very fulfilling for you.

Be a conduit for understanding among people. They can relate to each other easily through you. You can help them understand each other by explaining where each person is coming from.

LIFE AFFIRMATION: "I make choices that are right for me. The more I value myself, the greater my value to others."

Making choices that are right for you means saying no when you feel that your time and energy aren't being appreciated. For example, it may mean raising your fee to accurately reflect the value of the service you offer. When you sell yourself "cheap" (whether it's your time, energy, or service), you devalue yourself. When you do this, people don't value you. When you know your worth and treat it as a value, others will value it more, and there will be a more even exchange of energy.

ENERGY-BALANCING ACTIVITIES: (Refer to Appendix A at the end of Part Two for ideas.)

When you feel emotional: Earth activities
When you feel mentally stressed: Metal activities
When you feel burnt-out: Water activities
When you feel stuck: Wood activities
When you feel uninspired: Fire activities

SELENE ALCOR

Water + Metal

The Caring Perfectionist

Aka: The Sentimental Minimalist and The Adaptable Expert

PRIMARY ELEMENT: Water (Selene)

SECONDARY ELEMENT: Metal (Alcor)

YOUR OVERVIEW: As a Caring Perfectionist, you not only take responsibility for whatever you commit to, but you also put your heart and soul into it. You excel at learning from challenging situations and naturally create a new protocol for how to proceed more effectively in the future. You are a powerful source of both emotional and logical energy, and you thrive when you are put in situations that require you to be both creative and realistic. You have an engaging and charming personality, although maybe only a handful of people really know you. Connecting with others inspires you.

As a Sentimental Minimalist, you have the unique ability to show that you care without being overly emotional or verbal about it. As an Adaptable Expert, you are able to learn new ways to operate on the fly and can quickly master the ability to do something unfamiliar.

YOUR PURPOSE: You are here to manifest something bigger than yourself, and as a part of this manifestation, to facilitate connection between people.

YOUR CREED: "I follow the rules until I find another way that works better."

YOUR CORE DESIRE: To not overextend yourself and to be complete in all you do.

YOUR CORE VALUE: To make progress in whatever you're doing and be accepted for who you are.

AT YOUR BEST: You are articulate, introspective, self-contained, and enigmatic. Although you are realistic, you are willing to think outside the box. You are also reliable. You like to know people and help the people you know.

AT YOUR WORST: You overthink and look for the worst, have unwarranted insecurities, and are too critical and cautious as a result. You can be possessive, and you expect the worst rather than seeing the possibility of good.

YOUR ARCHETYPE TWIN: Metal + Water – Focused Visionary

MOST COMPATIBLE WITH:

Metal + Wood – Efficient Producer
Wood + Metal – Flexible Rule Maker

MOST SUPPORTED BY:

Metal + Earth – Masterful Ally
Earth + Metal – Reliable Analyst

MOST DRAINING FOR YOU:

Wood + Water – Logical Visionary
Water + Wood – Resourceful Creator

YOUR GREATEST TEACHER:

Earth + Fire – Loyal Cheerleader
Fire + Earth – Energetic Protector

YOUR ELEMENTAL DYNAMIC: Nurturing

Metal supports Water, so when you are balanced, you are able to effortlessly begin new projects and take them to completion. The Metal element within you helps you detach. The Water element within helps you stay connected.

However, since Water can drain Metal, when you are out of balance, you will experience nervousness and insecurity and lose your ability to stay connected, and then need to withdraw.

SUPPORTING ELEMENT: Earth

Earth supports the elements of Water and Metal. In the elemental cycle, Earth nurtures Metal, which in turn supports Water. The one element that supports both of your elements is Earth, so when you feel out of balance, being in Earth energy is extremely helpful. Hike, walk, ground yourself, or sit or lie on the floor. Physical touch like hugging is extremely grounding, so exchange hugs with those close to you. Getting a massage is very supportive, as well.

Having Earth elements in your environment is essential. Surround yourself with wall art depicting mountains, land, continents, stones, the planet Earth, as well as the earth tones you see outside. These are beneficial for Water/Metal Integrated Archetypes.

Earth energy is about strong foundations. It's about being certain and confident, so make it a point to spend time with people who have Earth as a part of their makeup (e.g., Talitha – Superhero Four).

YOUR PERSONAL VIRTUES:

Polished: You keep your motives and opinions to yourself until it's time to share, and when you do, people know your words were well-thought out.

Cautionary: You pause and think before you act. You point out things thoughtfully, helping to avoid errors and better navigate obstacles.

Subtly Powerful: You make people feel safe, and because of this, you subtly draw in others to join your point of view.

Perceptive: You know things because you feel the "vibes." You quickly understand the politics of a situation and the issues that concern others.

Discerning: You are both sensitive and intuitive, and you have great observational powers.

YOUR SUPERPOWERS:

Intuition, Connection, Focus, Commitment

WEAKNESSES TO STRENGTHEN:

Defensiveness, Insecurity, Faultfinding, Worry

YOUR MISSION FOR POWER:

Help others when the pressure is on. You excel when others are going through challenges because you are able show them how to calm down and take control of situations.

Forge bridges of understanding. You are sensitive to the feelings of others and able to quickly gauge the emotional tone of a room. Use your talents to make everyone feel comfortable. Showing your concern for others builds loyalty.

Offer support when others are going through challenges. You are a naturally strong and wise confidant. People will come to you with their needs and will also think of you when they see opportunities to help you.

Focus on a few things at a time. You function best when you can focus on your top priorities rather than operate in a broad and shallow way. Give yourself permission to reject projects or tasks that don't align with your overall vision and goals.

Take time for yourself. Even though you are able to accommodate others' needs, you need downtime, alone time, and reflection time. It's up to you to set boundaries on your time, otherwise you'll develop resentment.

LIFE AFFIRMATION: "My whole life has prepared me for what lies ahead. Everything I experience propels me towards my highest purpose."

Your Inner Archetype says: Life does not always go the way we wish. We all face disappointments, let-downs, and extremely challenging situations that don't always seem to make sense in the moment. And we often wonder, "*Why* did this happen to me?" Your life affirmation reminds you that, no matter what you experience, whether it's something good or an intense challenge, it's leading somewhere and is "not for naught." Life has given you what you need to move towards your highest purpose, which is to hone your skills and be the best person you can, your fears released and your greatest potential shining before you as you move your life toward more love, inspiration, and joy.

ENERGY-BALANCING ACTIVITIES: (Refer to Appendix A at the end of Part Two for ideas.)
When you feel emotional: Earth activities
When you feel mentally stressed: Metal activities
When you feel burned out: Water activities
When you feel stuck: Wood activities
When you feel uninspired: Fire activities

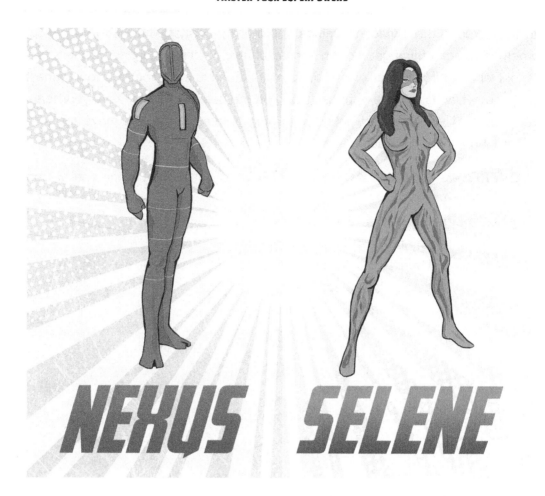

Wood + Water

The Logical Visionary

Aka: The Steadfast Magician and The Determined Nurturer

PRIMARY ELEMENT: Wood (Nexus)

SECONDARY ELEMENT: Water (Selene)

YOUR OVERVIEW: As a Logical Visionary, you are adept at using your heart and mind in everything, and you excel at making things happen. Due to your inherently curious nature, you've amassed a wealth of information that you love to share with others when called forth to do so. You are bold and direct when you need to be, yet are also able to adapt and be in the shadows when the situation calls for it. When you feel accomplished, you are especially creative.

People trust you because you make them feel safe. It's the way you make sense of life. Creativity, new information, and achievement inspire you. You will socialize if you know you have a role to play, but would prefer the company of a few close friends. People are drawn to you as a Steadfast Magician for your ability to consistently pull something out of a hat—your resources for information and people amaze them. As a Determined Nurturer, you place high importance on taking care of the people and things that have meaning to you.

YOUR PURPOSE: You are here to nurture your ideas and grow them beyond any limits that others place on you.

YOUR CREED: "As I achieve, I remember to experience every moment."

YOUR CORE DESIRE: To be yourself in life, and to be wanted and accepted for who you are.

YOUR CORE VALUE: To make progress in whatever you do, and to feel connected to the process and to everyone involved.

AT YOUR BEST: You are a hard worker, swift and efficient, yet you know how important it is for you to take breaks. You listen to reason, yet also know when your intuition is guiding you on a path that will serve you better. Secure in who you are, you can trust that everything uncertain and undetermined in your life will ultimately fall into place.

AT YOUR WORST: You are inflexible, judgmental, and hypersensitive to criticism. You move confidently to make decisions based on fear or you go into worry mode and feel unable to make a wise decision.

YOUR ARCHETYPE TWIN: Water + Wood – Resourceful Creator

MOST COMPATIBLE WITH:

Fire + Water – Radiant Provider

Water + Fire – Intuitive Luminary

MOST SUPPORTED BY:

Metal + Water – Focused Visionary

Water + Metal – Caring Perfectionist

MOST DRAINING FOR YOU:

Fire + Wood – Spontaneous Initiator

Wood + Fire – Innovative Idealist

YOUR GREATEST TEACHER:

Metal + Earth – Masterful Ally

Earth + Metal – Reliable Analyst

YOUR ELEMENTAL DYNAMIC: Nurturing

Water supports Wood, and together they work synergistically to stimulate growth. When you are in balance, you are creative, thriving, energetic, and make great progress on your goals. However, since Wood drains Water, it's important to take time to nurture both elements and not depend on Wood to be the energy generator and make all the progress.

In other words, if you are over-active with too much Wood energy (constantly on the go, striving for success, working on efficiency, focusing on productivity) without sufficient downtime for rest and reflection, which Water needs, you suffer from burnout. If, however, you are too laid back and drop out of active mode, you lack the stimulus you need to be successful in the way that you envision.

SUPPORTING ELEMENT: Metal

Metal acts as a support to the elements of Water and Wood. In the elemental cycle, Metal can transform itself into liquid (Water), which in turn fuels Wood. The one element both Water and Wood have as a support is Metal, so when you feel at odds with yourself, tired, or out of balance, it can be extremely helpful to bring Metal energy into your day. Get organized, write a To Do list, create a system, clear out physical and digital clutter, or get affairs in order. The more order you create, the more you'll find yourself coming into balance.

Having Metal elements in your environment is essential for support. Shiny metal objects, wall art depicting circular patterns, as well as pastels and the colors white and light grey are considered beneficial for Wood/Water Integrated Archetypes.

Metal energy is about precision and grace and drawing strong boundaries, so make it a point to spend time with individuals who have Metal as a part of their makeup (e.g., Alcor – Superhero Archetype Five).

YOUR PERSONAL VIRTUES:

Vibe-Sensitive: You are a smart thinker. You have the ability to quickly read the "vibes" of any situation and can even sense hidden agendas.

Agile: You have the ability to generate multiple solutions to a single problem and move quickly in a new direction when you need to.

Resourceful: You are able to come up with new ideas with little effort and intuitively know how to share your ideas in a way that people "get."

Prolific: You are an endless source of creative thought. Your inspired ideas flow forth freely.

Productive: You know how to get things done when it's time to get things done.

YOUR SUPERPOWERS:

Creativity, Adaptability, Intuition, Connection

WEAKNESSES TO STRENGTHEN:

Worry, Impatience, Insecurity, Defensiveness

YOUR MISSION FOR POWER:

Make people feel important. Whether talking to the cleaner, the grocery store bagger, or the CEO, show appreciation for what they do and how they do it. You'll make an engaging impression.

Leverage your knowledge. You are excellent at collecting and retaining information. Be open to using what you know to help others succeed. Sharing information with others will help you feel fulfilled.

Balance activity with passivity. You need to feel good, so schedule downtime along with active time and you will thrive. Being "unproductive" is restorative and necessary.

Use your sensitivity as a strength. Anticipate or prevent problems and see obstacles before they occur. When you sense that you are moving too fast or missing important details, consciously slow down and get back on track.

Share your dreams and goals. When you let others know where you are headed and what's important to you, they will rally around to help you succeed. Their expectations will also help to keep you going.

LIFE AFFIRMATION: "I am grateful for all things that happen in my life and know that I will soon see my challenges as my gifts."

If you are grateful, more is given. If you are not, more is taken away. Although there may be many things in your life that you don't feel thankful for and wish did not exist, your best bet for getting more of what you want is to hone your focus and master your thoughts by always looking for the upside. Just like a friend whose gift you did not show appreciation for, why would the Universe give you more gifts when you don't even appreciate the gifts you have already been given?

ENERGY-BALANCING ACTIVITIES: (Refer to Appendix A at the end of Part Two for ideas.)

When you feel emotional: Earth activities

When you feel mentally stressed: Metal activities

When you feel burned out: Water activities

When you feel stuck: Wood activities

When you feel uninspired: Fire activities

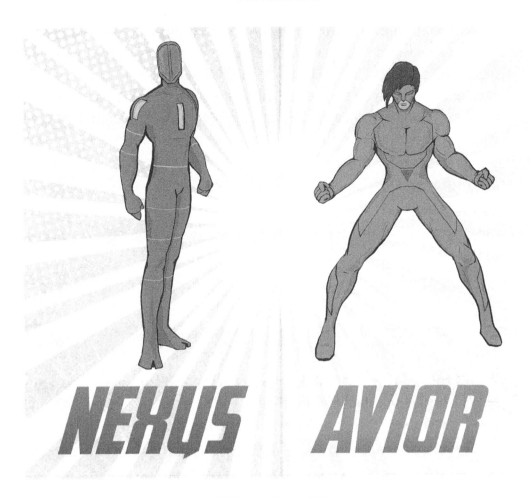

Wood + Fire

The Innovative Idealist

Aka: The Pioneering Adventurer and The Intelligent Charmer

PRIMARY ELEMENT: Wood (Nexus)

SECONDARY ELEMENT: Fire (Avior)

YOUR OVERVIEW: As an Innovative Idealist you find ways to make things happen, no matter how unconventional your ideas may be. You excel at communicating a vision and implementing the system that makes it happen, often to the surprise of others. You have a way of getting people to buy into what you believe without selling it to them. As an optimist and a magnetic source of energy, you thrive when you are efficiently getting things done and drawing others into the possibility that they also can achieve what they want in life.

Although it may take you some time to warm up in new situations or environments, you have a warm, welcoming, kind, and engaging personality. Ideas and heart-centered living inspire you. You delight in making life fun, and you know that, with dedication and desire, it can be better. People are drawn to you as a Pioneering Adventurer for your fearlessness in being the first to try something a bit risky. As an Intelligent Charmer, you know how to help people move through their fears and embrace life in new ways.

YOUR PURPOSE: You are here to show people what can be achieved when you follow your heart.

YOUR CREED: "Everything I want in life happens when I decide it's time to take action."

YOUR CORE DESIRE: To be comfortable being your authentic self, to inspire others, and to live a truly happy, heart-centered life.

YOUR CORE VALUE: To be efficient, productive, and organized—and happy along the way.

AT YOUR BEST: You are the embodiment of action and movement. You serve others by lifting them up when they most need it. You are accomplished, fair, and productive, and are able to be a great source of encouragement and celebration.

AT YOUR WORST: You are egotistic, detached, indecisive, and scattered. You get anxious and fearful that you won't accomplish what you set out to do.

YOUR ARCHETYPE TWIN: Fire + Wood – Spontaneous Initiator

MOST COMPATIBLE WITH:

Wood + Earth – Thriving Manifestor

Earth + Wood – Patient Speedster

MOST SUPPORTED BY:

Water + Wood – Resourceful Creator

Wood + Water – Logical Visionary

MOST DRAINING FOR YOU:

Fire + Water – Radiant Provider

Water + Fire – Intuitive Luminary

YOUR GREATEST TEACHER:

Water + Metal – Caring Perfectionist

Metal + Water – Focused Visionary

YOUR ELEMENTAL DYNAMIC: Nurturing

Wood supports Fire and together they create light, heat, and energy, so when you are in a state of balance, you are lighting up the world, generating positivity, and moving things forward. However, since Fire also consumes Wood, it's important to stay in balance by taking time to nurture both elements and not depend entirely on Wood to be the energy generator.

You'll experience frustration, impatience, and anger if you are over-active with too much Wood, which means you are taking too much time to plan, organize, talk, and think without incorporating enough spontaneity and leaving a bit to chance (which Fire needs). On the other hand, if you just go with whatever catches your attention without strategizing, you will lack the focus and control to be optimally productive and enthusiastic, and that will drain you.

SUPPORTING ELEMENT: Water

Water supports the elements of Fire and Wood. In the elemental cycle, Water nurtures Wood, which in turn fuels Fire. The only thing Fire and Wood have in common is Water, so when you feel at odds with yourself, tired, or out of balance, it is extremely helpful to be around Water energy, such as a pool, a spa, the ocean, a lake, or a waterfall.

Having Water in your environment is essential for support. Wall art depicting bodies of water and all shades of grey, charcoal, and black are considered beneficial for Wood/Fire Integrated Archetypes.

Water energy is about going with the flow and moving around obstacles without stress, so it can be helpful to make a point of spending time with individuals who have Water as a part of their makeup (e.g., Selene – Superhero Archetype One.)

YOUR PERSONAL VIRTUES:

Spontaneous: You are quick-witted and can think on your feet, whether in a personal, professional, or social situation.

Proactive: You are consistently able to step forward and take charge, especially when early action can make a big difference.

Vigorous: Working towards a goal energizes you. You are unfazed by deadlines and challenges and find ways to make your energy work for you.

Enterprising: You have the ability to see opportunity and turn it into success. You instigate new action and continually look to create new opportunities.

Forward-Thinking: You inspire others to look towards the future. You detest complacency and push yourself and others to innovate.

YOUR SUPERPOWERS:

Adaptability, Creativity, Positivity, Confidence

WEAKNESSES TO STRENGTHEN:

Worry, Impatience, Arrogance, Blame

YOUR MISSION FOR POWER:

Make sure you let people know that your optimism and positivity are not naivety; you know that bad things that are going on and are simply choosing to focus on the good.

Appreciate others and tell them how much they mean to you. You will not only make them feel better, but you will also expand the energy tank of your own well-being.

Protect your buoyant energy. Minimize your time with people who are not on the same page as you. When you feel tired and lethargic, ask yourself if you've outgrown some of the people you hang around with.

Be your own boss. You do best when you move at your own pace. Take time to be with others on your own schedule.

Recognize yourself and others. When you take the time for recognition, you will be more motivated in the next phase.

LIFE AFFIRMATION: "I powerfully manifest that which I desire by focusing specifically on what I want."

If you complain a lot, the Universe will respond lovingly and give you more to complain about. On the other hand, if you choose to look for what is going well, you will increase the chances that things will go smoothly. What you talk about or think about, you bring about. If you don't appreciate what you have, why would you get more to appreciate? Find more of what's good today so that you can experience more good in your life tomorrow.

ENERGY-BALANCING ACTIVITIES: (Refer to Appendix A at the end of Part Two for ideas.)

When you feel emotional: Earth activities

When you feel mentally stressed: Metal activities

When you feel burnt-out: Water activities

When you feel stuck: Wood activities

When you feel uninspired: Fire activities

NEXUS | TALITHA

Wood + Earth

The Thriving Manifestor

Aka: The Flexible Traditionalist and The Systematic Provider

PRIMARY ELEMENT: Wood (Nexus)

SECONDARY ELEMENT: Earth (Talitha)

YOUR OVERVIEW: Metamorphosis is your guiding principle as a Thriving Manifestor. You are driven by your desire to act and create change, especially when you know it ultimately helps others. Your enthusiasm and productivity are inspiring, and you excel when you are given free reign. Yet, you are also considerate and open to suggestions, allowing others to have input. When conflict arises, people look to you as the peacemaker, knowing that you can be the bridge and find solutions.

Togetherness, action, and harmony inspire you. You delight in working with others to move towards a unified goal. People are drawn to you as a Flexible Traditionalist for your conservative and realistic outlook, while they are also inspired by your ability to expand boundaries. As a Systematic Provider, you put everything in place to make sure that those you care about are supported in times of need.

YOUR PURPOSE: To encourage those you interact with daily to keep on going, no matter what obstacles they encounter.

YOUR CREED: "When I help others succeed, I succeed. When others are fulfilled, I am fulfilled."

YOUR CORE DESIRE: To comfortably be your authentic self and to live in peace and balance with minimal conflict.

YOUR CORE VALUE: To make progress in whatever you're doing and to ensure that everyone else is doing okay.

AT YOUR BEST: You are strong, yet flexible, and you perform well under stress. You are caring, but not overly gushy. You cover a lot of ground when you feel organized, making progress like no other.

AT YOUR WORST: You think too much and end up not progressing. You become restless and impatient when things take too long, and you get obsessed with your To Do list.

YOUR ARCHETYPE TWIN: Earth + Wood – Patient Speedster

MOST COMPATIBLE WITH:

Water + Metal – Caring Perfectionist

Metal + Water – Focused Visionary

MOST SUPPORTED BY:

Water + Fire – Intuitive Luminary

Fire + Water – Radiant Provider

MOST DRAINING FOR YOU:

Fire + Metal – Warm-Hearted Loner

Metal + Fire – Dedicated Enthusiast

YOUR GREATEST TEACHER:

Metal + Wood – Efficient Producer

Wood + Metal – Flexible Rule Maker

YOUR ELEMENTAL DYNAMIC: Controlling

Wood (think "tree") and Earth together create a foundation for productivity, growth, and manifestation, so when you are in a state of balance, you are stable and energetic and able to get things done. However, since Wood can also drain all the energy from Earth, it's important to take time to nurture both elements and not overdo one or the other.

If you are on the go too much (Wood energy) and don't give yourself enough routine, which Earth needs, you suffer from distraction and ineffectiveness. If, however, you get too comfortable (Earth), you get stuck, unable to break out of a rut, and you lack the stimulus you need to get things moving.

MISSING ELEMENT: Fire

Fire bridges the elements of Wood and Earth. In the elemental cycle, Wood nurtures Fire, which in turn becomes Earth. The only thing Wood and Earth have in common is Fire, so when you feel at odds with yourself, tired, or out of balance, it is extremely helpful to bring in Fire energy, which can be as simple as spending active time outdoors.

Having Fire elements in your environment is essential for support. Wall art depicting sunrises and all shades of the color red, purple, or orange are considered beneficial for Wood/Earth Integrated Archetypes.

Fire energy is about freedom and movement and being social and uninhibited, so it can be helpful to spend time with individuals who have Fire as a part of their makeup (e.g., Avior – Superhero Archetype Three).

YOUR PERSONAL VIRTUES:

Constructive: You have the ability to quickly scan a situation and know how to make it better. Once it is better, you look for ways to improve on it.

Creatively Practical: You always consider the risks of anything you do. Although you initially like to take the safe route, once comfortable, you'll think outside the box and get creative.

Curious: You delight in new information and new activity. You gather information and then assess how to move forward in a practical way.

Prolific: You have creative ideas that you act on as soon as you feel it's safe to do so. You are resourceful when it comes to dealing with obstacles, so you get a lot done.

Pioneering: You are always ready to challenge the current way and come up with new ways to reset the foundation for greater sustainability.

YOUR SUPERPOWERS:

Adaptability, Creativity, Patience, Consideration

WEAKNESSES TO STRENGTHEN:

Worry, Indecisiveness, Over-giving, Inability to say no

YOUR MISSION FOR POWER:

Live in the moment. Though you have a need for stability, remind yourself that the present is where your future is created. Your power lies in the inspired creativity you feel in each moment.

Reassure others often. Even though you are a mover and shaker, you have the ability to calm others in the midst of chaotic daily events, and they look to you as a protector.

Don't let others take advantage of your intrinsic ability to be flexible and giving. You do not need to compromise and bend to every whim of others.

Plan before taking action. You do best when you know where you are headed and how you are going to get there. Once you feel secure in the foundation, you will make much more progress than if you try to figure it out along the way.

Allow yourself necessary rejuvenation time. You have a need to be a couch potato from time to time and literally do nothing. Don't beat yourself up for being seemingly unproductive.

LIFE AFFIRMATION: "I make choices that are ultimately right for me, and by doing so I bring more balance to my life."

Never confuse selfishness with making choices that are right for you. The more you live your life according to what is best for you, the more joyful you become. Your happiness is the greatest possible gift to the Universe. When your heart is at peace and in a state of balance, it blesses everyone and everything it touches.

ENERGY-BALANCING ACTIVITIES: (Refer to Appendix A at the end of Part Two for ideas.)

When you feel emotional: Earth activities

When you feel mentally stressed: Metal activities

When you feel burnt-out: Water activities

When you feel stuck: Wood activities

When you feel uninspired: Fire activities

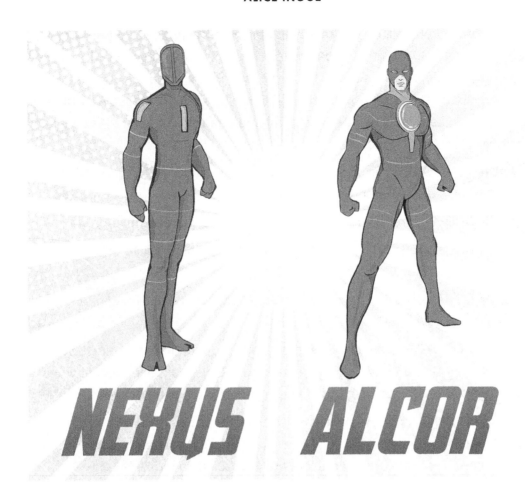

NEXUS | ALCOR

Wood + Metal

The Flexible Rule Maker

Aka: The Organized Professional and The Productive Authority

PRIMARY ELEMENT: Wood (Nexus)

SECONDARY ELEMENT: Metal (Alcor)

YOUR OVERVIEW: As a Flexible Rule Maker, you thrive when you are in a position to determine how things will get done while knowing that you have the option to change anything at any time. You excel at planning and action and have great strength in standing up for what you believe in, whether a person or a cause. You are an unwavering source of energy and thrive when you are able to achieve a goal or help someone else achieve theirs. You have a contemplative yet competitive personality.

Being in control inspires you, and you delight in being decisive (although you are not always so). You need separateness in any togetherness but will socialize if you have a role or a reason. As an Organized Professional, people are drawn to your methodical way of moving through to the finish. As a Productive Authority, you can seem lazy, but when it's time to meet a deadline, you know you have the resources to make it happen.

YOUR PURPOSE: You are here to set new standards for yourself and to transcend limits placed upon you by others.

YOUR CREED: "I reach my goals by being flexible, yet determined."

YOUR CORE DESIRE: To be yourself in life, and to complete everything you start.

YOUR CORE VALUE: To make progress in whatever you're doing, and to be organized along the way.

AT YOUR BEST: You are decisive, productive, independent, and direct, yet also can be a great support and help to others. You are pleasant and can converse in great depth, but you are also good at keeping your feelings to yourself.

AT YOUR WORST: You isolate, worry too much, and become critical of others, blaming them for things outside of your control. You become picky and have expectations of yourself and others that are impossible to meet.

YOUR ARCHETYPE TWIN: Metal + Wood – Efficient Producer

MOST COMPATIBLE WITH:

Earth + Fire – Loyal Cheerleader

Fire + Earth – Energetic Protector

MOST SUPPORTED BY:

Earth + Water – Calm Connector

Water + Earth – Reflective Confidant

MOST DRAINING FOR YOU:

Fire + Water – Radiant Provider

Water + Fire – Intuitive Luminary

YOUR GREATEST TEACHER:

Metal + Fire – Dedicated Enthusiast

Fire + Metal – Warm-Hearted Loner

YOUR ELEMENTAL DYNAMIC: Controlling

Metal and Wood together break things down (think of the metal blade of an axe chopping a tree), so when you are in balance, you are able to make a lot of progress and break up challenges or tasks into bite-size pieces for ease of forward movement.

However, since Wood can also destroy Metal, it's important to take time to nurture both elements and not overdo one or the other. If you move too quickly and don't take time to think things through, which is important to your Metal side, you'll suffer from self-judgment when things turn out less than acceptably by your standards, and you'll find it difficult to take confident future action. On the other hand, if you spend too much time trying to get every detail perfect, you won't get anywhere and will end up frustrated.

MISSING ELEMENT: Water

Water bridges the elements of Metal and Wood. In the elemental cycle, Metal transforms to Water (liquid), which in turn fuels Wood. The only thing Metal and Wood have in common is Water, so when you feel at odds with yourself, tired, or out of balance, Water energy, like swimming or being at a spa, is extremely helpful.

Having Water in your environment is essential for support. Wall art depicting bodies of water, as well as all shades of grey, charcoal, and black are considered beneficial for Wood/Metal Integrated Archetypes.

Water energy is about going with the flow and moving around obstacles without stress, so it can be helpful to make a point of spending time with individuals who have Water as a part of their makeup (e.g., Selene – Superhero Archetype One).

YOUR PERSONAL VIRTUES:

Intentional: You know what you want when you set out to do it. You move and communicate with clear purpose.

Orderly: You can organize and present in a no-nonsense way. You are able to create platforms from which to be efficient.

Astute: You are quickly able to assess situations. After getting familiar, you are able to see the key issues and help make a plan to move forward.

Logical: You make decisions by weighing the pros and cons. When you do anything or make any decision, you look for the upsides and downsides. You probably even create a checklist.

Insightful: You communicate your ideas with clarity and conviction. People trust you because, when you are certain, you are confident and sharp.

YOUR SUPERPOWERS:

Adaptability, Creativity, Focus, Commitment

WEAKNESSES TO STRENGTHEN:

Worry, Impatience, Faultfinding, Inflexibility

YOUR MISSION FOR POWER:

Work toward productive flexibility. You are adaptable by nature, and yet you still resist sudden change. Greater flexibility will ensure that your progress towards goals is second to none.

After each success, take time to reflect on how and why you won. You are self-competitive and like to win, and you can learn more from winning than from losing.

Learn to analyze the past and find the positive. When you do so, you can be known as an active agent for positive change. This is a natural expertise for you.

Establish order in your life. If you feel frustrated because you are not productive, take time to purchase some organizational systems. Order is necessary for you. You need to have a place for everything in your environment to support optimal progress.

Look beyond how others do things when you have to deal with people who operate differently. Not everyone thinks like you or does things like you. Keep your focus on getting to the goal.

LIFE AFFIRMATION: "It's okay to live a life that no one understands. The more I accept myself, the happier I am."

Sometimes you want to do things that you know others won't approve of. When you respect or care about what those people think and do what they want you to do, you end up living a life that doesn't feel like your own. When you try to explain yourself, you are met with judgment or disapproval. This can make you feel quite unhappy. Remember, your life is yours to live. Understand that you have different needs and wants than others. Choose to be bold and do or be what you want. It will be hard at first, but the more you understand that you are being who you need to be, you can be happy no matter what others think.

ENERGY-BALANCING ACTIVITIES: (Refer to Appendix A at the end of Part Two for ideas.)

When you feel emotional: Earth activities

When you feel mentally stressed: Metal activities

When you feel burnt-out: Water activities

When you feel stuck: Wood activities

When you feel uninspired: Fire activities

Fire + Water

The Radiant Provider

Aka: The Brilliant Resource and The Extroverted Introvert

PRIMARY ELEMENT: Fire (Avior)

SECONDARY ELEMENT: Water (Selene)

YOUR OVERVIEW: As a Radiant Provider, you are a seemingly endless source of positive energy when it comes to providing others with what they need. You excel at nurturing an idea or a person, and your presence alone can give people hope even on their darkest days. You thrive when you are needed, wanted, and welcomed, and will go out of your way to make sure someone you care about is taken care of in every way possible.

You are warm and have a contagious, expressive, and fun-loving personality. Although you don't seek outward recognition, appreciation from others inspires you to go above and beyond the call of duty. People are drawn to you as a Brilliant Resource for your intuitive ability to connect them with the right resource at the right time. As an Extroverted Introvert, you are open, friendly, and social, but you really do need time away from people and activities in order to recharge.

YOUR PURPOSE: You are here to pioneer new paths by following your intuition and transcending what the world has told you is not possible.

YOUR CREED: "I allow my inner voice to illuminate my life's journey."

YOUR CORE DESIRE: To live a fun, happy life without compromising yourself, your time, or your energy.

YOUR CORE VALUE: To follow your heart and to be able to do what inspires you in life.

AT YOUR BEST: You are self-motivated, confident, and energetic. You are able to listen to and connect with people. You can be the center of attention or anonymous and feel great either way. You know how to create your own fun when necessary, so you can be alone or enjoy company.

AT YOUR WORST: You are insecure and moody, either seeking attention or withdrawing. You fear the worst, anticipate calamity, and exaggerate negative possibilities.

YOUR ARCHETYPE TWIN: Water + Fire – Intuitive Luminary

MOST COMPATIBLE WITH:

Metal + Earth – Masterful Ally

Earth + Metal – Reliable Analyst

MOST SUPPORTED BY:

Metal + Wood – Efficient Producer

Wood + Metal – Flexible Rule Maker

MOST DRAINING FOR YOU:

Wood + Earth – Thriving Manifestor

Earth + Wood – Patient Speedster

YOUR GREATEST TEACHER:

Earth + Water – Calm Connector

Water + Earth – Endearing Peacemaker

YOUR ELEMENTAL DYNAMIC: Controlling

Fire and Water together create steam, so you are powerful and dynamic when balanced. However, since Fire can also be put out by Water, it's important to nurture both elements and not overdo one or the other.

If you are too active and don't get enough downtime for rest and rejuvenation, which Water needs, you suffer from depletion and burnout. If, on the other hand, you spend too much time alone, you lack the stimulus you need to be creative and inspired.

MISSING ELEMENT: Wood

Wood bridges the elements of Water and Fire. In the elemental cycle, Water nurtures Wood, which in turn fuels Fire. The only thing Water and Fire have in common is Wood, so when you feel at odds with yourself, tired, or out of balance, being in "Wood" energy, like nature, is extremely helpful.

Having plants (real or silk) in your environment is essential for support. Wall art depicting nature along with all shades of green are considered beneficial for Fire/Water Integrated Archetypes.

Wood energy is about moving forward and being adaptable, so it can be helpful to make a point of spending time with individuals who have Wood as a part of their makeup (Nexus – Superhero Archetype Two).

YOUR PERSONAL VIRTUES:

Catalyzing: You are an out-of-the-box person and you dislike structure, so when everyone else gets stuck, you can think of exciting ideas to precipitate a new direction.

Calmly Energizing: You are calm and yet you energize others. If something becomes too routine or habitual, you are able to challenge or to help reinvent it.

Alluring: You have a great personality and others warm to you quite naturally. You communicate in a way that draws them in.

Subtly Dramatic: You speak and mesmerize others in an understated way that keeps them intrigued. You captivate them with what you have to say.

Entrepreneurial: You have ideas and aren't afraid to try them out. You can start new projects and implement new plans with enthusiasm.

YOUR SUPERPOWERS:

Positivity, Confidence, Intuition, Connection

WEAKNESSES TO STRENGTHEN:

Negativity, Arrogance, Insecurity, Defensiveness

YOUR MISSION FOR POWER:

Help others succeed. Seek opportunities where you can assist people to get to the next level. You have the ability to show people their strengths and walk them through their fears.

Trust in your ideas. You may have ideas and goals that are loftier and brighter than most are used to. If something feels right in your heart, no matter what others may or may not say, trust your intuition and move forward.

Highlight the positive. You tend to be more positive and enthusiastic than most people. When others are hesitant to take risks, your attitude can help them move forward. People look to you to lift them up.

Make sure you take time to rest. Even though you have the energy to keep on going, your mood and well-being depend on your ability to recharge. Self-time is essential and non-negotiable.

Share your experiences and stories. People rely on you to help them rise above their daily challenges and feel better. When others are down, be ready to tell them a story of something you've gone through that they can relate to.

LIFE AFFIRMATION: "No one can take away the love in my heart and the wisdom I have gained. These make up the magnificence of who I am."

When you feel down, remember this—no one can take from you these two things: the love you have in your heart and the wisdom you have gained over the years. When you feel challenged, you may feel you've lost these two things. If you're feeling this way, it's helpful to remember that even the most terrible events in your past have brought you gifts that are useful in the present. Right now, you have inside you the two things you most need to fulfill your life—love and wisdom. Get back to affirming what you *do* have. Warm your spirit by refocusing your thoughts and feelings on the magnificence of your being.

ENERGY-BALANCING ACTIVITIES: (Refer to Appendix A at the end of Part Two for ideas.)

When you feel emotional: Earth activities

When you feel mentally stressed: Metal activities

When you feel burnt-out: Water activities

When you feel stuck: Wood activities

When you feel uninspired: Fire activities

Fire + Wood

The Spontaneous Initiator

Aka: The Inspired Trailblazer and The Optimistic Doer

PRIMARY ELEMENT: Fire (Avior)

SECONDARY ELEMENT: Wood (Nexus)

YOUR OVERVIEW: As a Spontaneous Initiator, you confidently take action on ideas and desires the moment they pop into your head. You excel at getting things started and have a way of mobilizing others to get going, even if they are not in the mood. You are an endless source of energy and ideas, and you thrive when you are on the go, getting things done, helping others, and being productive. You have an infectious personality, and people want to hang around you because being with you rejuvenates them.

Creativity, fun, and happiness inspire you. You delight in movement, growth, and spontaneity. You know that you can turn ideas into action. If you can improve the world at the same time, you are further motivated. As an Inspired Trailblazer, you draw people to you through your pioneering spirit. As an Optimistic Doer, you look to what's possible and surprise people with your attitude of finding the positives in a situation, even if they are challenging.

YOUR PURPOSE: You are here to lift the spirits of fellow human beings and show others what's possible to achieve in life.

YOUR CREED: "If I love it, I can find a way to have it or do it."

YOUR CORE DESIRE: To inspire others, and experience each moment of life all while being able to be your authentic self.

YOUR CORE VALUE: To be happy, efficient, and productive.

AT YOUR BEST: You are courageous, self-motivated, and creative, and your life is organized in a way that others don't really understand. You are dynamic and knowledgeable about many things, and you pride yourself on being able to do it all yourself, without asking for help.

AT YOUR WORST: You waste time on meaningless tasks, are quick-tempered, impatient, blunt, and quick to anger. Your impulsiveness and impatience lead to activity and movement that doesn't get anything tangible done.

YOUR ARCHETYPE TWIN: Wood + Fire – Innovative Idealist

MOST COMPATIBLE WITH:

Wood + Earth – Thriving Manifestor

Earth + Wood – Patient Speedster

MOST SUPPORTED BY:

Water + Wood – Resourceful Creator

Wood + Water – Logical Visionary

MOST DRAINING FOR YOU:

Fire + Water – Radiant Provider

Water + Fire – Intuitive Luminary

YOUR GREATEST TEACHER:

Water + Metal – Caring Perfectionist

Metal + Water – Focused Visionary

YOUR ELEMENTAL DYNAMIC: Nurturing

Wood supports Fire and together they create light, heat, and energy, so when you are in balance, you light up the world, generating positivity and moving things forward. However, since Wood can also be consumed by Fire, it's important to nurture both elements to remain in balance and not depend on Wood to be the energy generator.

You'll experience frustration, impatience, and anger when you are over-active with too much Wood, which means you are taking too much time to plan, organize, talk, and think. Fire needs spontaneity and a bit of chance. On the other hand, if you just go with whatever catches your attention without strategizing, you will lack the focus and control you need to be optimally productive and enthusiastic, and that will drain you.

SUPPORTING ELEMENT: Water

Water supports the elements of Fire and Wood. In the elemental cycle, Water nurtures Wood, which in turn fuels Fire. The only thing Fire and Wood have in common is Water, so when you feel at odds with yourself, tired, or out of balance, being around Water energy (pools, spas, the ocean, waterfalls) is extremely helpful.

Having Water in your environment as well is essential for support. Wall art depicting bodies of water as well all shades of grey, charcoal, and black are considered beneficial for Fire/Wood Integrated Archetypes.

Water energy is about going with the flow and moving around obstacles without stress, so it will be helpful to spend time with individuals who have Water as a part of their makeup (e.g., Selene – Superhero Archetype One).

YOUR PERSONAL VIRTUES:

Captivating: You are naturally brilliant in the way you present yourself. You captivate others with the depth of your conviction.

Energetic: You are a storehouse of energy, and your presence inspires others to enjoy life more.

Motivated: You are motivated in ways others want to be, and people look up to you for inspiration.

In-the-know: You are informed on the latest of anything relevant and interesting, and you are sought after for this trait. Your expertise about what you know is inspiring.

Desirable: You are wanted at the center of everything. People naturally gravitate toward you to hear what you have to say. They enjoy your charm.

YOUR SUPERPOWERS:

Positivity, Confidence, Adaptability, Creativity

WEAKNESSES TO STRENGTHEN:

Negativity, Arrogance, Impatience, Indecisiveness

YOUR MISSION FOR POWER:

Create timelines and deadlines for whatever you commit to. Because you love being busy and relish being on the go, it's important to determine when you will finish so you don't overdo.

Celebrate your success when you finish something significant. Since you tend to move on quickly to the next thing, it's important for you to build self-value by consciously pausing and appreciating what you have done.

Set demanding goals for yourself. It's easy for you to act, so just make sure it's serving a purpose and helping you to evolve.

Openly share your challenges. People may think that your life is all roses because of your optimism. Make sure that you let them know that you have difficulties, as well. You make the most difference when people see that you are human, too.

Insulate yourself from negativity. Just because you are upbeat doesn't mean that people and situations can't drag you down. Consistently choose who you hang out with and make sure they are of the same "vibe" so that you don't get worn out.

LIFE AFFIRMATION: "I allow the enlightened part of me to be my guide rather than the part of me that fears a negative outcome."

Like all of us, you have two parts. The core of who you are is trusting, loving, fearless, visionary, and balanced, and it is the pure essence of love. You have another part that protects you. Some call it the ego, and it likes to look at the downside. It brings up all the things that could go wrong, that might go wrong, and that need to be guarded and defended against. When you live your life listening to this voice in your head, you limit yourself. You play safe and small, and it doesn't feel good. Use this affirmation as a reminder to listen to the voice of possibilities and love.

ENERGY-BALANCING ACTIVITIES: (Refer to Appendix A at the end of Part Two for ideas.)

When you feel emotional: Earth activities

When you feel mentally stressed: Metal activities

When you feel burned out: Water activities

When you feel stuck: Wood activities

When you feel uninspired: Fire activities

AVIOR TALITHA

Fire + Earth

The Energetic Protector

Aka: The Pleasure-Seeking Diplomat and The Enthusiastic Giver

PRIMARY ELEMENT: Fire (Avior)

SECONDARY ELEMENT: Earth (Talitha)

YOUR OVERVIEW: As an Energetic Protector, you are "all in" when it comes to taking care of anything you consider *yours*—whether a person, a project, or a cause. You excel at being expressive, engaging, and spontaneous while also making others feel that you are dependable and can be trusted. You are a positive source of nurturing energy. You thrive when you have the opportunity to build lasting relationships and create things of value. You have a naturally helpful and loyal personality, and you light up when you are celebrated and appreciated for your efforts.

Action is what inspires you. You delight in considering all the best options before taking a chance, but once you decide, you are unstoppable! As a Pleasure-Seeking Diplomat, you are effortlessly the ambassador of fun. People are drawn to you, and you bring them together for enjoyable causes. As an Enthusiastic Giver, you give whenever you can, and when you do, you give abundantly and joyfully.

YOUR PURPOSE: You are here to show others that it's possible to stand up for yourself while also being kind and considerate.

YOUR CREED: "Life is best when enjoyed and experienced with those I care about."

YOUR CORE DESIRE: To do what makes you happy and stay connected with those you care about.

YOUR CORE VALUE: To enjoy all the moments of life without having to sacrifice your own desires.

AT YOUR BEST: You are strong-willed and competitive, while also understanding and selfless. You are the perfect mix of proactive and cautionary. Energizing and sociable, when you turn on your charm you quickly build relationships you sustain over time by making the people feel heard and valued.

AT YOUR WORST: You are stubborn, impatient, egotistical, and over-valuing of yourself but can also bend to please, becoming a doormat when you do not trust in your own abilities and values.

YOUR ARCHETYPE TWIN: Earth + Fire – Loyal Cheerleader

MOST COMPATIBLE WITH:

Metal + Fire – Dedicated Enthusiast

Fire + Metal – Warm-Hearted Loner

MOST SUPPORTED BY:

Wood + Fire – Innovative Idealist

Fire + Wood – Spontaneous Initiator

MOST DRAINING FOR YOU:

Earth + Metal – Reliable Analyst

Metal + Earth – Masterful Ally

YOUR GREATEST TEACHER:

Water + Wood – Resourceful Creator

Wood + Water – Logical Visionary

YOUR ELEMENTAL DYNAMIC: Nurturing

Fire supports Earth, and together they create a fertile foundation. When you are in balance, you energize and sustain yourself and create from a strong foundation. However, since Earth can also drain Fire, it's important to take time to nurture both elements and not depend only on Fire to be the energy generator.

If you have too much Fire activity (on the go all the time) and not enough reflection and rejuvenation, which Earth needs, you will suffer from burnout and energy drain. But if you lack the stimulus you need to be creative, you will be unproductive, stuck in an uncomfortable state of inertia.

SUPPORTING ELEMENT: Wood

Wood supports the element of Earth through Fire. In the elemental cycle, Wood fuels Fire, which in turn produces Earth. Since Fire and Earth are supported by Wood, when you feel at odds with yourself, tired, or out of balance, being in Wood energy, like nature, is extremely helpful.

Having plants (real or silk) in your environment is essential for support. Wall art depicting nature as well as all shades of the color green are considered beneficial for Fire/Earth Integrated Archetypes.

Wood energy is about moving forward and being adaptable, so making it a point to spend time with individuals who have Wood as a part of their makeup (Nexus – Superhero Archetype Two) can be helpful.

YOUR PERSONAL VIRTUES:

Competent: You are strong-minded and unfazed by setbacks. When you are confident in your ability, you surprise others with your proficiency and power.

Charming: When you turn on your charm, you are able to quickly build relationships and make people feel comfortable.

Inclusive: You have the ability to get everyone involved in anything you are inspired by and draw them into the fold.

Immediate: Though you consider your actions and reactions, you work hard to avoid delay. You can get things going, and get things done on time.

Protective: You are loyal to the people, places, and things for which you take responsibility. You help when there is challenge and excel in initiating well-being for all.

YOUR SUPERPOWERS:

Positivity, Confidence, Patience, Consideration

WEAKNESSES TO STRENGTHEN:

Negativity, Blame, Difficulty saying no, Over-giving

YOUR MISSION FOR POWER:

Catalyze situations and people. Look for ways to help others take action. They will be grateful for your energy, and you will feel fulfilled.

Remember that you learn from real experience. Whenever you can, get away from theory; to build your foundation, go out and consciously expose yourself to challenges that will test your skills and knowledge.

Earn trust and loyalty first. In certain situations, you can come across as over-enthusiastic and impatient to get started. Remember that sometimes your effectiveness comes from tempering your impulsiveness.

Energize the plans and ideas of others. Your energy can bring them to completion, and you can build value with people who have ideas that need to get off the ground.

Make sure you give reasons. You have more enthusiasm than most, so when you try to motivate others, give them a reason to do what you say. Bring in your practical side.

LIFE AFFIRMATION: "I focus on where things are going right, even when they're not perfect. I appreciate what I have and I get more to appreciate."

When things are not going the way we want them to, we tend to complain and blame. This is natural. For example, when you get together with friends, you tell each other everything that's going wrong. The more you do this, the more incomplete is the picture you paint of the situation and the more difficulties you attract. What you think about, you bring about. And what you focus on, you attract more of. Let this affirmation remind you to look for what *is* going right—so you can receive more to celebrate! When you take your eyes off the obstacles, you will naturally see a new path on which you can move forward.

ENERGY-BALANCING ACTIVITIES: (Refer to Appendix A at the end of Part Two for ideas.)

When you feel emotional: Earth activities

When you feel mentally stressed: Metal activities

When you feel burnt-out: Water activities

When you feel stuck: Wood activities

When you feel uninspired: Fire activities

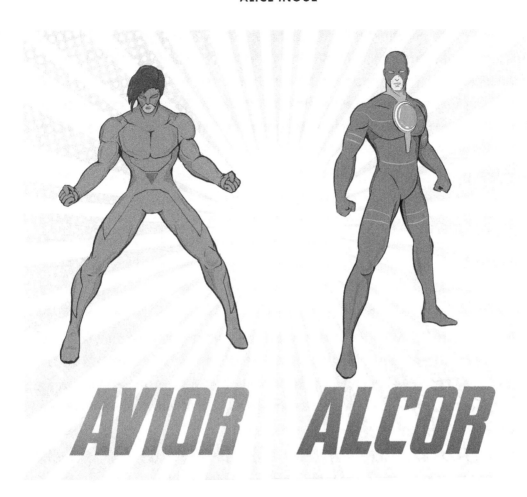

Fire + Metal

The Warm-Hearted Loner

Aka: The Dynamic Master and The Expressive Connoisseur

PRIMARY ELEMENT: Fire (Avior)

SECONDARY ELEMENT: Metal (Alcor)

YOUR OVERVIEW: As a Warm-Hearted Loner, you enjoy spending time socializing and connecting, yet you also love contemplative alone time. You are a vibrant source of energy and thrive when you are being sought after for your expertise. When people get to know you, they see that underneath the fun and playful exterior is a person who is serious about life, has an analytical side, and maintains self-imposed high standards.

You fascinate people with your ability to remain graceful and composed under pressure. Connection inspires you—whether with groups of people or with bodies of knowledge. As a Dynamic Master, your enthusiasm and ability to learn things quickly draws people to you. As an Expressive Connoisseur, you openly share everything you are passionate about and are respected as an expert in anything that interests you.

YOUR PURPOSE: You are here to encourage others to discover their heartfelt direction and to inspire them to dedicate themselves to it.

YOUR CREED: "Even when the odds are stacked against me, I can achieve."

YOUR CORE DESIRE: To have fun in life but still complete what you are committed to.

YOUR CORE VALUE: To experience what life has to offer while still being efficient.

AT YOUR BEST: You are dynamic, engaging, and outgoing, and yet you temper your expression with grace and style. Though generous, you can be analytically pragmatic and careful about how you spend your resources. You take risks that are quite calculated and have a steely determination about anything you put your heart into.

AT YOUR WORST: You are arrogant, egotistical, and judge others excessively for their shortcomings. Anxious, picky, and needing to maintain control, you tend to boss people around. You swing from being overly cautious to being unable to control your excesses.

YOUR ARCHETYPE TWIN: Metal + Fire – Dedicated Enthusiast

MOST COMPATIBLE WITH:

Water + Wood – Resourceful Creator

Wood + Water – Logical Visionary

MOST SUPPORTED BY:

Earth + Wood – Patient Speedster

Wood + Earth – Thriving Manifestor

MOST DRAINING FOR YOU:

Earth + Water – Calm Connector

Water + Earth – Reflective Confidant

YOUR GREATEST TEACHER:

Water + Fire – Intuitive Luminary

Fire + Water – Radiant Provider

YOUR ELEMENTAL DYNAMIC: Controlling

Fire and Metal together can move obstacles. Think how Fire can turn a hard element like Metal into liquid. When you are in balance, you have the unique ability to transform old structures into new forms. However, since Metal also can be destroyed by Fire, it's important to nurture both elements and not overdo one or the other.

If you are overactive with too much emphasis on Fire (socializing, being out and about, and doing too much), you suffer from ineffectiveness and burnout. Metal needs downtime for contemplation, restoration, and peace. However, if you spend too much time analyzing and thinking by yourself without enough social contact, you lack the stimulus you need to make progress.

MISSING ELEMENT: Earth

Earth bridges the elements of Water and Metal. In the elemental cycle, Fire turns into Earth, which brings forth Metal. The one element that supports both of your elements is Earth, so when you feel out of balance, being in Earth energy is extremely helpful. This means hiking, walking, grounding yourself, and sitting or lying on the floor. Hugging and physical touch with those close to you is extremely grounding, and getting a massage is supportive, as well.

Having Earth elements in your environment is essential. Surround yourself with wall art depicting mountains, land, continents, stones, and the planet Earth, as well as earth tones that you see when you look outdoors. These are beneficial for Fire/ Metal Integrated Archetypes.

Earth energy is about strong foundations. It's about being certain and confident, so it can be helpful to make a point of spending time with individuals who have Earth as a part of their makeup (e.g., Talitha – Superhero Four).

YOUR PERSONAL VIRTUES:

Ambitious: Your constant drive to improve keeps your standards high both for yourself and for others.

Focused: You can home in on a goal that is important to you and stay positive on the way to achieving it.

Confident: You are self-assured in ways that the average person is not, and because of this, you can surpass your own goals.

Complex: You can be both warm and cool, approachable when necessary and detached when the situation calls for it.

Dynamic: You get energized by working towards a goal. You love getting ready for what you have been planning.

YOUR SUPERPOWERS:

Positivity, Confidence, Focus, Commitment

WEAKNESSES TO STRENGTHEN:

Negativity, Impatience, Worry, Faultfinding

YOUR MISSION FOR POWER:

Be strategic in how you use your energy. You have the ability to create motion and momentum in others. Make sure you are wise about where you "spend" it so you don't overextend.

Practice how you confront others. You have the ability to stand up for what you believe in. Cultivate your style so that you can subtly persuade others to follow.

Ask people for their opinions. At times you can forget that there are other ways to look at things besides your own. It can help you to be open to other viewpoints.

Take charge when you can. You have the ability to lead and to calm others in times of crisis. Use your talents to reassure them and to let them know you have things under control.

LIFE AFFIRMATION: "I accept both the positive and the negative aspects of my life. In doing so, I find deep peace, balance, and stability."

Think back to the most recent crisis in your life. Did it feel like your whole world had stopped? Did you feel emotionally crazy? How long did it take to regain your balance? The faster you are able to see the blessing in any situation, the better you will feel. Everything challenging in our lives ultimately contains hidden blessings that reveal themselves in time. If you can see the good in a crisis right away, your healing journey will be faster and much less emotionally draining. That's why it's important to focus on accepting the blessings and benefits in every challenging situation that occurs. Use your life affirmation to help you find peace and balance.

ENERGY-BALANCING ACTIVITIES: (Refer to Appendix A at the end of Part Two for ideas.)

When you feel emotional: Earth activities

When you feel mentally stressed: Metal activities

When you feel burnt-out: Water activities

When you feel stuck: Wood activities

When you feel uninspired: Fire activities

TALITHA SELENE

Earth + Water

The Calm Connector

Aka: The Considerate Reflector and The Trusting Magician

PRIMARY ELEMENT: Earth (Talitha)

SECONDARY ELEMENT: Water (Selene)

YOUR OVERVIEW: As a Calm Connector, you make people feel cared for, safe, and valued. You excel at minimizing conflict and keeping the peace, and you have the ability to easily garner the trust of others. You are a great listener; people feel heard when they are with you. You are a steadfast source of calming energy, and you thrive when you are following your intuition. You have a caring personality, but you are able to stand your ground when it comes to something you really believe in.

Connecting people to products, thoughts, themselves, or other people inspires you. You delight in being the one who gives people the knowledge or opportunity to find a new path. You thrive when you follow your heart. Your ability as a Considerate Reflector to offer people ways to make their lives better draws them to you. As a Trusting Magician, you give people hope that miracles can happen, even to them.

YOUR PURPOSE: You are here to find yourself and to fully honor and value who you are.

YOUR CREED: "I am loyal to that which nurtures my soul."

YOUR CORE DESIRE: To make sure everyone is happy but not overextend yourself.

YOUR CORE VALUE: To live peacefully and with minimal conflict.

AT YOUR BEST: You are gentle, intuitive, wise, and creative. You speak up when you have a strong opinion and accept people for who they are without judging. You are thoughtful, considerate, and able to connect with others on a very human level.

AT YOUR WORST: You hold on to physical things, people, mindsets, and ideas long after they have stopped serving you. You subordinate to others' opinions and rules and lose your sense of a center. You are either passively stubborn and ignore what needs to be taken care of or you procrastinate and neglect what you know you need to do.

YOUR ARCHETYPE TWIN: Water + Earth – Reflective Confidant

MOST COMPATIBLE WITH:

Fire + Wood – Spontaneous Initiator

Wood + Fire – Innovative Idealist

MOST SUPPORTED BY:

Fire + Metal – Warm-Hearted Loner

Metal+ Fire – Dedicated Enthusiast

MOST DRAINING FOR YOU:

Water + Metal – Caring Perfectionist

Metal + Water – Focused Visionary

YOUR GREATEST TEACHER:

Water + Fire – Intuitive Luminary

Fire + Water – Radiant Provider

YOUR ELEMENTAL DYNAMIC: Controlling

Earth and Water together create stability, so when you are in balance, you are poised and calm. However, since Earth can also slow the flow of Water, it's important to take time to nurture both elements and not overdo one or the other.

If Earth energy begins to dominate, you feel stuck in a rut, unable to move forward in new and dynamic ways. If there is too much Water energy and not enough Earth, which Water needs to keep it from draining away, you lose your center and are not able to draw strong boundaries around your time and energy.

MISSING ELEMENT: Metal

Metal bridges the elements of Earth and Water. In the elemental cycle, Earth produces Metal, which when heated turns into liquid (Water). The only thing Earth and Water have in common is Metal, so when you feel at odds with yourself, drained, stuck, or out of balance, it can be extremely helpful to bring Metal energy into your day. This might involve getting organized, writing a To Do list, creating a system, clearing out both physical and digital clutter, or getting your affairs in order. The more order you create, the more balance you'll experience.

Having Metal elements in your environment is essential for support. Shiny metal objects, wall art depicting circular patterns, as well as pastels and the colors white and light grey are considered beneficial for Earth/Water Integrated Archetypes.

Metal energy is about precision and grace and drawing strong boundaries, so it can be helpful to make a point of spending time with individuals who have Metal as a part of their makeup (e.g., Alcor – Superhero Archetype Five).

YOUR PERSONAL VIRTUES:

Safe: You naturally make others feel safe in your presence. No matter how challenging the situation, they feel calm when you are present.

Thorough: Whatever you commit to, you see it through to the end. Because of your caring nature, you slow down when others interfere, but you eventually finish things up.

Reliable: It's not in your nature to let people down. You have standards when it comes to family, friends, and commitments.

Balancing: You bridge people and communities by neutralizing polarity. When two people are at odds, you are able to see both sides and connect to both with understanding.

Devoted: You are dedicated to the people and projects to which you are committed. You tend to stick with people who've been with you throughout your journey.

YOUR SUPERPOWERS:

Patience, Consideration, Intuition, Connection

WEAKNESSES TO STRENGTHEN:

Difficulty saying no, Over-giving, Insecurity, Defensiveness

YOUR MISSION FOR POWER:

Recall your positive impact on people. When you feel overwhelmed, think about how you've influenced others' lives, and it will remind you of your value. This will rejuvenate your drive to complete your commitments.

Build connections with those who are independent and have strong focus. When you need expertise, be open to advice from such people, as they can help you see other valuable perspectives.

Draw people together when there is conflict. When you are mitigating conflict, ask others to share their thoughts. You have the ability to be the harmonizer and move things in a different direction.

Practice ways to stand strong without confrontation. It's not natural for you to speak up, so prepare by learning techniques, otherwise you'll resort to passive-aggressive behavior.

Let your caring nature show, even in professional environments. Build connections by finding people to help or mentor. Don't hesitate to reach out and ask others to help you; they will, because you so gladly help others.

LIFE AFFIRMATION: "I say no when I need to. By doing so, I value myself and my time and save myself from future pain."

It's always best to do or say what you want. If you don't do what you know inside is right, you will keep attracting unwanted, energy-draining lessons. For example, if you don't say no to someone who keeps asking for your time and energy but doesn't appreciate it, you will attract increasingly greater frustration until you finally get the "lesson" and say no, anyway. Let's not be out-of-truth in our words and actions. Learn to say no in a graceful and loving way. Read the above affirmation often for strength and to prepare for the future.

ENERGY-BALANCING ACTIVITIES: (Refer to Appendix A at the end of Part Two for ideas.)

When you feel emotional: Earth activities

When you feel mentally stressed: Metal activities

When you feel burnt-out: Water activities

When you feel stuck: Wood activities

When you feel uninspired: Fire activities

TALITHA NEXUS

Earth + Wood

The Patient Speedster

Aka: The Faithful Communicator and The Grounded Inventor

PRIMARY ELEMENT: Earth (Talitha)

SECONDARY ELEMENT: Wood (Nexus)

YOUR OVERVIEW: As a Patient Speedster, before you do anything important, even if you feel like you can't wait, you consider everything and move forward only when you are comfortable with the path. You excel at commitment and organization and will do everything it takes to make sure you've anticipated and planned for the unknown. You are a steady source of upbeat energy and thrive when you feel safe and secure. Although conservative in some ways, you are willing to take calculated risks. You have a warm, caring, and engaging personality, but you can go into "all-business" mode when you need to.

Progress and productivity inspire you. You delight in creating new out of old. You know that your greatest value lies in being realistic, yet optimistic. Your loyalty and dedication as a Faithful Communicator draw people to you. As a Grounded Inventor, you think outside the box, but do it in a way that makes people feel safe with your ideas.

YOUR PURPOSE: You are here to nourish and support others in their growth, all while surpassing your own expectations of self.

YOUR CREED: "I experience success when I assist others in reaching their goals."

YOUR CORE DESIRE: To live in peace and balance with minimal conflict, and to comfortably be your authentic self without compromise.

YOUR CORE VALUE: To make sure those around you are taken care of and to be progressive.

AT YOUR BEST: You are adaptable, yet systematic and organized and extremely productive. You are calm, dependable, and supportive and are able to provide a safe place for others to confide in you. You are able to provide wise insight and direction when ideas are needed.

AT YOUR WORST: You procrastinate, get stuck in a rut, and become frustrated with yourself for not changing in a way you know is good for you. You worry excessively about situations, don't speak up when you are angry, and over-accommodate to keep the peace.

YOUR ARCHETYPE TWIN: Wood + Earth – Thriving Manifestor

MOST COMPATIBLE WITH:

Water + Metal – Caring Perfectionist

Metal + Water – Focused Visionary

MOST SUPPORTED BY:

Water + Fire – Intuitive Luminary

Fire + Water – Radiant Provider

MOST DRAINING FOR YOU:

Fire + Metal – Warm-Hearted Loner

Metal + Fire – Dedicated Enthusiast

YOUR GREATEST TEACHER:

Metal + Wood – Efficient Producer

Wood + Metal – Flexible Rule Maker

YOUR ELEMENTAL DYNAMIC: Controlling

Together, Wood (think "tree") and Earth create a foundation for productivity, growth, and manifestation, so when you are in a balanced state, you are stable and energetic and able to get things done. However, since Wood can also drain all the energy from Earth, it's important to take time to nurture both elements and not overdo one or the other.

If you are on the go too much (Wood energy) and don't give yourself enough routine, which Earth needs, you suffer from distraction and ineffectiveness. If, however, you get too comfortable (Earth), you get stuck and are unable to break out of ruts because you lack the stimulus you need to get things moving.

MISSING ELEMENT: Fire

Fire bridges the elements of Wood and Earth. In the elemental cycle, Wood nurtures Fire, which in turn becomes Earth. The only thing Wood and Earth have in common is Fire, so when you feel at odds with yourself, tired, or out of balance, it can be extremely helpful to be around Fire energy, which can be as simple as spending some active time outdoors.

Having Fire elements in your environment is essential for support. Wall art depicting sunrises and all shades of the color red, purple, or orange are considered beneficial for Earth/Wood Integrated Archetypes.

Fire energy is about freedom and movement, about being social and uninhibited, so it can be helpful to make a point of spending time with individuals who have Fire as a part of their makeup (e.g., Avior – Superhero Archetype Three).

YOUR PERSONAL VIRTUES:

Straightforward: You communicate your ideas with clarity and enthusiasm. You have a no-nonsense yet delightful approach to life.

Hardworking: You are guided by personal principles that lead you to put your time and energy into that which you desire to manifest.

Capable: No one questions your ability to get things done. You not only deliver results, but you also exceed expectations.

Principled: Even when there are obstacles, you stay on course. You don't want to let others down, so you find creative ways to make things work.

Purposeful: You don't act rashly or randomly, and over time, people know they can depend on you for your balanced, yet creative approach.

YOUR SUPERPOWERS:

Patient, Considerate, Adaptable, Creative

WEAKNESSES TO STRENGTHEN:

Difficulty saying no, Giving too much, Indecisiveness, Judgmentalism

YOUR MISSION FOR POWER:

Do what you say you're going to do. What you say every day builds your credibility. Others will notice your commitment to consistency, and you will reap long-lasting benefits.

Help others feel better about the not-so-good things that happen. Use this ability to help others see and understand the rationale behind challenges to their peace.

Push yourself to say no once in a while. You like to please, you like to "be doing," and at times you overextend. Remind yourself that it's okay to say no.

Partner with people who are focused. You bring the energy, perseverance, and commitment to any endeavor, and when you know where you're going, you excel and are valued.

Make sure rules and responsibilities are clear. Anytime you are going to collaborate, make sure there is clarity as to who is responsible for what so that you don't shoulder most of the workload and build resentment.

LIFE AFFIRMATION: "Whenever I need something to further my purpose, synchronistic situations align for me to get exactly what I want."

At this very moment, things are coming together for you in ways that are not yet apparent. Everything you want is in the process of becoming a reality. A lot goes on behind the scenes to make this happen. So, whenever you are frustrated or things are not unfolding as quickly as you'd like, stop and notice what *is* happening. Notice all the synchronicities you actually experience each day. See how some things *do* happen at the right time and *do* come together in the right way. Even if small, these are all signs to let you know that you are on the right track. Use this affirmation to help you remember that everything is falling into place.

ENERGY-BALANCING ACTIVITIES: (Refer to Appendix A at the end of Part Two for ideas.)

When you feel emotional: Earth activities

When you feel mentally stressed: Metal activities

When you feel burnt-out: Water activities

When you feel stuck: Wood activities

When you feel uninspired: Fire activities

Earth + Fire

The Loyal Cheerleader

Aka: The Responsible Fun-Lover and The Devoted Hero

PRIMARY ELEMENT: Earth (Talitha)

SECONDARY ELEMENT: Fire (Avior)

YOUR OVERVIEW: As a Loyal Cheerleader, once you decide to commit to a person, project, event, or cause, you put your energy into it and stay devoted to the end. You excel at understanding the needs of others and have the ability to rally resources and offer positive encouragement to help others feel secure. You intuitively know how to make people feel better and are a steadfast and vibrant source of energy. You thrive when you are enthusiastically working towards a goal. Others turn to you when they need someone who is encouraging and understanding.

Being in harmony with others energizes you, and when there is no conflict and you are in a state of balance, you are tireless in pursuit of your goals. As a Responsible Fun-Lover, you're the perfect mix of adult and child—you love having fun but make sure that no one is left out or uncomfortable with the activity. As a Devoted Hero, you consistently show others that you are looking out for them, constantly saving the day by showing support when it is most needed.

YOUR PURPOSE: You are here to encourage others to follow their heartfelt dreams and to be the foundation upon which they can feel safe to do so.

YOUR CREED: "Keeping the peace is better at times than being right."

YOUR CORE DESIRE: To be there for the people you care about, yet still do what makes you happy in life.

YOUR CORE VALUE: To enjoy all the moments of life without having to sacrifice your own desires in order to keep the peace.

AT YOUR BEST: You are tactful and self-sufficient, mindful, organized, and logical, yet still willing to go out on a limb, take a chance on life, and take advantage of unexpected opportunities. You can be in the spotlight if you have to be and yet are perfectly willing to be a silent support.

AT YOUR WORST: You are scattered and indecisive. You play the martyr and overextend yourself. You become over-anxious about minor things, get stuck, feeling unable to move forward.

YOUR ARCHETYPE TWIN: Fire + Earth – Energetic Producer

MOST COMPATIBLE WITH:

Metal + Fire – Dedicated Enthusiast

Fire + Metal – Warm-Hearted Loner

MOST SUPPORTED BY:

Wood + Fire – Innovative Idealist

Fire + Wood – Spontaneous Initiator

MOST DRAINING FOR YOU:

Earth + Metal – Reliable Analyst

Metal + Earth – Masterful Ally

YOUR GREATEST TEACHER:

Water + Wood – Resourceful Creator

Wood + Water – Logical Visionary

YOUR ELEMENTAL DYNAMIC: Nurturing

Fire supports Earth and together they create a fertile foundation, so when you are in balance, you have energy to sustain yourself and create from a strong foundation. However, since Earth can also suffocate Fire, it's important to take time to nurture both elements and not depend on Fire to be the energy generator.

If you are overactive with too much Fire activity (on the go all the time) and not enough reflection and rejuvenation, which Earth needs, you suffer from burnout and energy drain. If however, you lack the stimulus you need to be creative, you will get stuck in an uncomfortable state of inertia that leaves you unproductive.

SUPPORTING ELEMENT: Wood

Wood supports the element of Earth through Fire. In the elemental cycle, Wood fuels Fire, which in turn produces Earth. Since Fire and Earth are supported by Wood, when you feel at odds with yourself, tired, or out of balance, it is extremely helpful for you to be in Wood energy, as in nature.

Having plants (real or silk) in your environment is essential for support. Wall art depicting nature as well as all shades of the color green are considered beneficial for Earth/Fire Integrated Archetypes.

Wood energy is about moving forward and being adaptable, so make it a point to spend time with individuals who have Wood as a part of their makeup (Nexus – Superhero Archetype Two).

YOUR PERSONAL VIRTUES:

Helpful: You are genuine and sincere; others feel your warmth and authenticity. You are someone people can always ask for help.

Tireless: You are determined in your pursuit of what you believe in and what you want to accomplish. You have boundless energy when you want to get something done.

Protective: You are watchful over people and projects to make sure that nothing goes wrong. People are loyal to you because you go out of your way to take care of them.

Prepared: You anticipate problems and prepare for them, yet you also are prepared to tackle the unexpected and conquer. You are literally prepared for anything.

Conscientious: You are diligent for two reasons: one, because you like to be thorough, thoughtful, and considerate; and two, because you don't want to lose face by letting others down.

YOUR SUPERPOWERS:

Patience, Consideration, Positivity, Confidence

WEAKNESSES TO STRENGTHEN:

Bending to please others, Giving too much, Arrogance, Negativity

YOUR MISSION FOR POWER:

Remember that what you do inspires others. Share your support and resources so others can find their way when things are down for them. Let people know how you find your joy.

Encourage others whenever you can. Your ability to be sincere in your praise helps others accept what you say as truth. Intentionally learn as much as you can about the people you meet, as this will catalyze trusting relationships.

Recognize your ability to relate to people. **Speak** often about your purpose of motivating others to find their own sense of direction. When you relate to people, they feel understood.

Take action to balance yourself. Make sure you set aside time for activity and fun with others as well as time for nurturing yourself. In order for you to operate from power and at your best, you need to feel balanced,

Take note when others are successful. When you notice that someone has accomplished something, praise them and be specific in your praise about what you noticed. The more specific you are about what you observe led to their success, the more you enhance their growth.

LIFE AFFIRMATION: "I spend my time, money, resources, and energy wisely. I am productive and bring the best of who I am to the table of life."

The more you affirm what you want, and the clearer you are about how you want to spend your time, money, and energy, the more you will use those resources to your advantage. It always feels good to operate in a balanced way—not overly extravagant and yet not miserly, either. You do your best and feel your best when you are in a state of balance. You are more patient, loving, and understanding. And, when you act from your center, you also make better choices in life.

ENERGY-BALANCING ACTIVITIES: (Refer to Appendix A at the end of Part Two for ideas.)

When you feel emotional: Earth activities

When you feel mentally stressed: Metal activities

When you feel burnt-out: Water activities

When you feel stuck: Wood activities

When you feel uninspired: Fire activities

TALITHA ALCOR

Earth + Metal

The Reliable Analyst

Aka: The Comforting Alchemist and The Dependable Thinker

PRIMARY ELEMENT: Earth (Talitha)

SECONDARY ELEMENT: Metal (Alcor)

YOUR OVERVIEW: As a Reliable Analyst, you prefer to take the time to consider all options before rushing into anything. You excel at reassurance and thoughtfulness, and you inspire others to do their best work. Soft-spoken, yet confident, you thrive when you are in control and are able to move at your own pace. You are level-headed and unfazed by setbacks, but you just don't like surprises that throw you completely off track. You have a warm yet introverted personality and care deeply about the people close to you.

People are drawn to you as a Comforting Alchemist because of your ability to help them "magically" feel better when they are with you, especially when they are worried about something. As a Dependable Thinker, you are someone people feel they can trust because they know that you care enough to take their problems seriously.

YOUR PURPOSE: You are here to encourage others to trust in the power of planning and patience.

YOUR CREED: "When things need to happen, they will."

YOUR CORE DESIRE: To help others with their needs but still stay focused on your own goals.

YOUR CORE VALUE: To be caring and inclusive of others while holding strong boundaries around your time and energy.

AT YOUR BEST: You are caring and giving, yet also know how to set firm boundaries. You are incredibly resourceful, rational, and precise, and you love to share your ideas. You are methodical and steadfast and produce quality results.

AT YOUR WORST: You can be stubborn, lethargic, and overly critical. You become overly needy and uncertain and stop expressing yourself. First you blame yourself and then you blame others and allow resentment to build. You sway from over-subordinating yourself to others to being cool and distancing yourself.

YOUR ARCHETYPE TWIN: Metal + Earth – Masterful Ally

MOST COMPATIBLE WITH:

Water + Earth – Reflective Confidant

Earth + Water – Calm Connector

MOST SUPPORTED BY:

Fire + Earth – Energetic Protector

Earth + Fire – Loyal Cheerleader

MOST DRAINING FOR YOU:

Water + Metal – Caring Perfectionist

Metal + Water – Focused Visionary

YOUR GREATEST TEACHER:

Wood + Fire – Innovative Idealist

Fire + Wood – Spontaneous Initiator

YOUR ELEMENTAL DYNAMIC: Nurturing

Earth supports Metal and together they create sustainability. Like that, when you are in balance, you are resilient, unshakeable. However, since Metal also drains Earth, it's important to nurture both elements and not depend on Earth to be the energy generator.

If too much emphasis is placed on Earth qualities (staying safe, being compassionate and conservative) and not enough on Metal qualities (being creative and open to change), which Metal thrives on, you suffer from stagnation and lack of progress. If, however, you are over-controlling, you shut off the flow you need to attain your personal goals.

SUPPORTING ELEMENT: Fire

Fire supports the elements of Metal and Earth. In the elemental cycle, Fire produces Earth, which in turn cultivates Metal. Fire is the element that supports and connects Metal through Earth, so when you feel at odds with yourself, tired, or out of balance, being in Fire energy is extremely helpful. That can be as simple as spending some active time outdoors.

Having Fire elements in your environment is essential for support. Wall art depicting sunrises and all shades of the colors red, purple, or orange are considered beneficial for Earth/Metal Integrated Archetypes.

Fire energy is about freedom and movement, about being social and uninhibited, so it can be helpful to spend time with individuals who have Fire as a part of their makeup (e.g., Avior – Superhero Archetype Three).

YOUR PERSONAL VIRTUES:

Constant: Your ability to be stable is significant because you can keep your cool even when there is a setback. People know what to expect from you, and they rely on you.

Balanced: When faced with an important decision, you use intuition and rationale to your advantage

Magnetic: You pull people in because of your ability to hold back information and details, yet at the same time make them feel close and connected.

Unobtrusive: You get things done without needing to draw attention to yourself and your achievements. You are competitive but do it without flaunting.

Pragmatic: You are logical and practical and able to consider all resources and possibilities as you plan for maximum ease.

YOUR SUPERPOWERS:

Patience, Consideration, Focus, Commitment

WEAKNESSES TO STRENGTHEN:

Difficulty saying no, Procrastination, Worry, Inflexibility

YOUR MISSION FOR POWER:

Share your values and what's important to you with others. This will help them understand and relate to you better.

Be honest with people when they ask for your feedback. Although you have strong opinions, you have the ability to say things with grace. This is to your advantage and will build trust.

Put yourself out there. You usually wait to sense if it's "safe" before you open up fully. Remember, your engaging nature and genuineness draw people in, so bring out your shine first!

Connect with people to thrive. Make time for close friends with whom you feel grounded and happy.

Get clarity to ground yourself. No matter what situation you are in, don't hold back from asking questions, even though you find it easier to say nothing to avoid bringing attention to yourself. You thrive when matters are clear.

LIFE AFFIRMATION: "I surround myself with people who affect my life positively and gently release those who drain my energy."

It is easy to get into habits, hanging out with the same people and doing the same things because you feel you "should" without understanding that you are not in a positive environment. Instead of thinking that you can handle it, it's good to realize that you can choose who you hang out with. If you can't extricate yourself because it's your work or family, then limit the amount of time you spend with those people. You need to have people around you who influence your day and your path in a positive way.

ENERGY-BALANCING ACTIVITIES: (Refer to Appendix A at the end of Part Two for ideas.)

When you feel emotional: Earth activities

When you feel mentally stressed: Metal activities

When you feel burnt-out: Water activities

When you feel stuck: Wood activities

When you feel uninspired: Fire activities

Metal + Water

The Focused Visionary

Aka: The Structured Intuitive and The Conscientious Philosopher

PRIMARY ELEMENT: Metal (Alcor)

SECONDARY ELEMENT: Water (Selene)

YOUR OVERVIEW: As a Focused Visionary, you can efficiently and effectively bring anything into manifestation when you see it clearly in your mind's eye. You offer a graceful yet powerful source of energy to any endeavor, and you thrive when you are contributing with your extraordinarily creative mind. You like being connected to others but are selective as to who you allow close to you.

When something doesn't feel right, you know you can make it better. You are loyal and willing to support anything or anyone who has gained your respect.

You are considerate and thoughtful and shy away from conflict. When you are not appreciated or valued, you tend to disconnect. People are drawn to you as a Structured Intuitive for your ability to read situations for what they are. As a Conscientious Philosopher, you have the capacity to talk about concepts while still relating to reality.

YOUR PURPOSE: You are here to use your innate creativity and depth of experience to create a life and lifestyle that are authentic to who you are.

YOUR CREED: "Let's maintain separateness in our togetherness."

YOUR CORE DESIRE: To be needed by others, but not so much that it takes away from your plans and focus on what you want in life.

YOUR CORE VALUE: To be efficient, and to be valued for what you contribute.

AT YOUR BEST: You are firm and precise, yet flexible and understanding. You are resilient and able to come up with solutions even when under pressure.

AT YOUR WORST: You are detached, critical, controlling, and intolerant. You get emotional and then withdraw without communicating your true feelings.

YOUR ARCHETYPE TWIN: Water + Metal – Caring Perfectionist

MOST COMPATIBLE WITH:

Metal + Wood – Efficient Producer

Wood + Metal – Flexible Rule Maker

MOST SUPPORTED BY:

Metal + Earth – Masterful Ally

Earth + Metal – Reliable Analyst

MOST DRAINING FOR YOU:

Wood + Water – Logical Visionary

Water + Wood – Resourceful Creator

YOUR GREATEST TEACHER:

Earth + Fire – Loyal Cheerleader

Fire + Earth – Energetic Protector

YOUR ELEMENTAL DYNAMIC: Nurturing

Metal supports Water, and so, when you are balanced, you are able to effortlessly begin new projects and take them to completion. The Metal element within you helps you detach. The Water element within helps you stay connected.

However, since Metal can be eroded by Water, when you are out of balance, you will experience nervousness and insecurity, lose your ability to stay connected, and feel the need to withdraw.

SUPPORTING ELEMENT: Earth

Earth supports the elements of Water and Metal. In the elemental cycle, Earth nurtures Metal, which in turn supports Water. The one element that supports both of your elements is Earth, so when you feel out of balance, being in Earth energy is extremely helpful. This means hiking, walking, grounding yourself, and sitting or lying on the floor. Hugging and physical touch with those close to you is extremely grounding. Getting a massage is very supportive, as well.

Having Earth elements in your environment is essential. Surround yourself with wall art depicting mountains, land, continents, stones, and the planet Earth as well as earth tones that you find outside in nature. These are beneficial for Metal/Water Integrated Archetypes.

Earth energy is about strong foundations. It's about being certain and confident, so it can be helpful to make a point of spending time with individuals who have Earth as a part of their makeup (e.g., Talitha – Superhero Four).

YOUR PERSONAL VIRTUES:

Selective: You carefully consider your decisions and are not automatically sold on a new idea or way of doing things.

Efficient: You care about people but also know how to stay on track. You pair empathy with practicality.

Elegant: You bring a subtle yet understated dedication to anything you do. You choose your words carefully, your emails are refined, and you impress people with your style.

Discreet: You gain others' trust by your ability to operate silently, yet effectively. You're not driven by ego as much as by your ability to listen.

Distinguished: You know what you are looking for. You carefully choose your words and approach, and you excel at picking just the right ideas to present to anyone.

YOUR SUPERPOWERS:

Focus, Commitment, Intuition, Connection

WEAKNESSES TO STRENGTHEN:

Worry, Inflexibility, Insecurity, Defensiveness

YOUR MISSION FOR POWER:

Solve problems where you can. Let people know that they can come to you when they are having a problem. Your desire to help others, combined with your intuitive nature, fuels your ability to formulate solutions for others, which you find fulfilling.

Share your calmness and certainty. When things are chaotic, it's easy for those involved to worry and get distracted. Letting others know that everything is going to be okay helps them to feel comforted and secure.

Be candid. You can become known as a source of truth by seizing opportunities to speak about sensitive subjects and bringing up delicate issues. You have the ability to see things clearly and speak in a way that is not offensive to others.

Accept that you will make mistakes. Mistakes trouble you because being "perfect" is a core part of who you are. Keeping your expectations of yourself and others realistic is the best attitude to adopt.

Trust your intuition. You are observant and may pick up on things that others don't. Make sure to speak up; your hunches may be valuable when you bring them to the attention of those you know are receptive to them.

LIFE AFFIRMATION: "My life is coming together in perfect alignment. Any fears I have are an imperfect view of an incomplete reality."

Whenever we really want something, we naturally put up our defenses, think negatively, and fear the worst—because, after all, what if we don't get it? This way we won't be disappointed. It's natural to think like this. It's easy to imagine a one-sided reality in which what you want doesn't exist, when in fact there are more sides to consider than just the negative! Because people are negative by nature, we tend not to consider the positive side of what could be coming together, so this affirmation is a great reminder that everything is going to be all right.

ENERGY-BALANCING ACTIVITIES: (Refer to Appendix A at the end of Part Two for ideas.)

When you feel emotional: Earth activities

When you feel mentally stressed: Metal activities

When you feel burnt-out: Water activities

When you feel stuck: Wood activities

When you feel uninspired: Fire activities

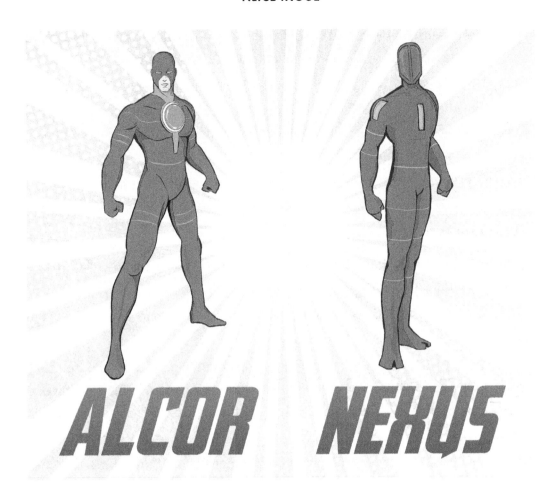

Metal + Wood

The Efficient Producer

Aka: The Refined Warrior and The Disciplined Planner

PRIMARY ELEMENT: Metal (Alcor)

SECONDARY ELEMENT: Wood (Nexus)

YOUR OVERVIEW: As an Efficient Producer, you thrive when you find systems that accelerate your productivity. You excel at making things happen and holding yourself or others accountable. You can find the energy to do anything when it comes to what you believe in.

You are a steadfast source of energy to others and thrive when you are making progress and feeling organized. Your personality is such that you like to follow your own rules, although you are willing to be open and entertain what others have to say. Knowledge inspires you. You delight in learning new ways to do old things and excel at finding information to improve things for you and others.

People are drawn to you as a Refined Warrior for your graceful yet firm desire to come out ahead. As a Disciplined Planner, you begin preparing the moment you are certain there needs to be a plan, but you also can make changes at the last minute when you are confident of success.

YOUR PURPOSE: You are here to contribute to others by creating platforms that support any person, project, or cause you believe in.

YOUR CREED: "If I make a plan, I can do anything."

YOUR CORE DESIRE: To be uncompromisingly who you are and efficient and productive at the same time.

YOUR CORE VALUE: To make progress in life by getting things done and moving on.

AT YOUR BEST: You are kind, steady, understanding, and gentle. You take responsibility and operate well independently. You are good at taking the time to understand how things work and are able to push things to the limit to seek out the best or to be the best.

AT YOUR WORST: You are unforgiving, impatient, and intolerant. You lose your sense of humor when you are frustrated by too many obstacles. You end up thinking too much and are unable to decide, and then you get aggravated with either yourself or others.

YOUR ARCHETYPE TWIN: Wood + Metal – Flexible Rule Maker

MOST COMPATIBLE WITH:

Earth + Fire – Loyal Cheerleader

Fire + Earth – Energetic Protector

MOST SUPPORTED BY:

Earth + Water – Calm Connector

Water + Earth – Reflective Confidant

MOST DRAINING FOR YOU:

Fire + Water – Radiant Provider

Water + Fire – Intuitive Luminary

YOUR GREATEST TEACHER:

Metal + Fire – Dedicated Enthusiast

Fire + Metal – Warm-Hearted Loner

YOUR ELEMENTAL DYNAMIC: Controlling

Together, Metal and Wood break things down (think of the metal blade of an axe chopping Wood), so when you are in balance, you are able to make a lot of progress, breaking challenges or tasks into bite-size pieces for ease of forward movement.

However, since Wood also can be destroyed by Metal, it's important to take time to nurture both elements and not overdo one or the other. If you move too quickly and don't take the time to think things through, which is important to your Metal side, you'll suffer from negative self-judgment when things turn out less than acceptably, and that will make it hard for you to take confident future action. If, however, you spend too much time trying to get every detail perfect, you'll not get anywhere and end up frustrated.

MISSING ELEMENT: Water

Water bridges the elements of Metal and Wood. In the elemental cycle, Metal transforms to Water (liquid), which in turn fuels Wood. The only thing Metal and Wood have in common is Water, so when you feel at odds with yourself, tired, or out of balance, you need Water energy, like swimming or going to a spa.

Having Water in your environment is essential for support. Wall art depicting bodies of Water as well as all shades of grey, charcoal, and black are considered beneficial for Metal/Wood Integrated Archetypes.

Water energy is about going with the flow and moving around obstacles without stress, so it can be helpful to make a point of spending time with individuals who have Water as a part of their makeup (e.g., Selene – Superhero Archetype One).

YOUR PERSONAL VIRTUES:

Standard-Setter: You like to set high standards for yourself and others. You raise the bar of every endeavor, every project, and every interaction.

Reasoned: You act with intention, not irrationality. You work hard, do things with purpose, and bring common sense to any situation.

On-Target: You love clarity and getting to the point. You are detailed and bring focused clarity to groups and situations.

Systematic: In your pursuit of perfection, you don't leave things to chance. Your work and your life are organized and measured.

Dignified: You respond to problems with reasoning, and once something makes sense to you, you communicate with grace and confidence.

YOUR SUPERPOWERS:

Focus, Commitment, Adaptability, Creativity

WEAKNESSES TO STRENGTHEN:

Faultfinding, Impatience, Indecisiveness, Worry

YOUR MISSION FOR POWER:

Concentrate on your priorities. You do best when you restrict your focus to only a few initiatives and demands. Give yourself permission to reject everything else that is offered. This will build your credibility with others, who will trust your sense of value.

Seek roles where you can operate independently. Although you can work with others, you function best when you stay on your own track and don't allow others to distract you.

Give quantity and quality equal voice. No matter what you are doing, you feel best when you take both quantity and quality into consideration. This leads to solid results and productivity that is fulfilling.

Look for new information to stimulate you. You grow by learning, whether the knowledge is immediately useful or not. As your mind is open and absorbent, you can nurture yourself by reading, scanning the internet, and allowing your curiosity free rein. You'll gain respect as someone with wise resources.

Identify your greatest talents and value. Once you know what you both love and are naturally good at, refine your skills. For your greatest happiness in life, practice and work toward establishing a few strategic areas of strength.

LIFE AFFIRMATION: "My perspective is completely in my control. My power lies in seeing my challenges as positive benefits."

When we are challenged by something, all we can think about is how bad it is, which prompts us to look for all the disadvantages and find more to support the negativity we feel. This results in a warped view and a horrible feeling inside. You suffer. You may think you can't help it, but actually, you can. You can do it by being conscious. During challenging times, it helps to remember that you can look at what is happening from other perspectives. Choose the ones that make you feel better, not worse.

ENERGY-BALANCING ACTIVITIES: (Refer to Appendix A at the end of Part Two for ideas.)

When you feel emotional: Earth activities

When you feel mentally stressed: Metal activities

When you feel burnt-out: Water activities

When you feel stuck: Wood activities

When you feel uninspired: Fire activities

ALCOR **AVIOR**

Metal + Fire

The Dedicated Enthusiast

Aka: The Refined Superstar and The Gifted Wizard

PRIMARY ELEMENT: Metal (Alcor)

SECONDARY ELEMENT: Fire (Avior)

YOUR OVERVIEW: As a Dedicated Enthusiast, you know it's important to take time to contemplate any situation before you fully commit, but once you decide to move forward on something, you are unstoppable. You keep your standards high in all that you do and operate with heart and enthusiasm. You are a unique combination of someone who is a good listener as well as someone people look to for inspiration.

You have an enigmatic personality, and you love being respected and acknowledged for what you know. You are self-competitive, constantly striving to reach higher. As a Refined Superstar, you have a humble yet confident personality. As a Gifted Wizard, you delight others with your creativity at the most unexpected times, whether it's a brilliant idea or a resourceful connection.

YOUR PURPOSE: You are here to move through barriers and obstacles and by doing so, to show others that it's all about heart.

YOUR CREED: "When I decide it's worth my time to do something, I will succeed."

YOUR CORE DESIRE: To stay focused on your goals while also having fun.

YOUR CORE VALUE: To be responsible, yet still able to let go and experience what life offers.

AT YOUR BEST: You are enigmatic and the perfect mix of reserved yet dramatic and conservative yet bold, drawing others in with your ability to gracefully entertain them. You are approachable and able to make others feel secure with you. You make quick connections that serve you later.

AT YOUR WORST: You are arrogant and overconfident, which leads to impulsive actions you later regret. You want to be in control, overdoing and overanalyzing everything, which drives others crazy and gets nothing accomplished. When you are worried, you become inflexible, and that detracts from your natural gift of creativity.

YOUR ARCHETYPE TWIN: Fire + Metal – Warm-Hearted Loner

MOST COMPATIBLE WITH:

Water + Wood – Resourceful Creator

Wood + Water – Logical Visionary

MOST SUPPORTED BY:

Earth + Wood – Patient Speedster

Wood + Earth – Thriving Manifestor

MOST DRAINING FOR YOU:

Earth + Water – Calm Connector

Water + Earth – Reflective Confidant

YOUR GREATEST TEACHER:

Water + Fire – Intuitive Luminary

Fire + Water – Radiant Provider

YOUR ELEMENTAL DYNAMIC: Controlling

Fire and Metal together can move obstacles. (Consider how Fire can turn a hard element like Metal into liquid). Therefore, when you are in balance, you have the unique ability to transform old structures into new forms. However, since Metal also can be destroyed by Fire, it's important to take time to nurture both elements and not overdo one or the other.

If you are overactive with too much emphasis on Fire (socializing, being out and about and doing too much) and not enough downtime for restoration, peace, and contemplation, which Metal needs, you suffer from ineffectiveness and burnout. On the other hand, if you spend too much time analyzing and thinking in solitude without enough social contact, you lack the stimulus you need to make progress.

MISSING ELEMENT: Earth

Earth bridges the elements of Water and Metal. In the elemental cycle, Fire turns into Earth, which brings forth Metal. The one element that supports both of your elements is Earth, so when you feel out of balance, being in Earth energy is extremely helpful: hiking, walking, grounding yourself, and sitting or lying on the floor. Hugging and having physical touch with those close to you is extremely grounding. Getting a massage is also very supportive.

Having Earth elements in your environment is essential. It is beneficial for you as a Metal/Fire Integrated Archetype to surround yourself with wall art depicting mountains, land, continents, stones, or the planet Earth, as well as earth tones that you see outside in nature.

Earth energy is about strong foundations, about being certain and confident, so it can be helpful to spend time with individuals who have Earth as a part of their makeup (e.g., Talitha – Superhero Four).

YOUR PERSONAL VIRTUES:

Dedicated: You invigorate others to work tirelessly at whatever they say they want to do. People realize you are in their corner. Your positive attitude is inspiring.

Intriguing: You hold your cards close so others don't know what you are thinking, but then, when it is least expected, you show how thoroughly you've thought through everything.

Observant: You are aware of surroundings and people. You are attentive and alert and recognize the red flags that warn something is at risk.

Leading: You are a natural leader, able to gather people around you and come forth with a plan for success.

Results-Oriented: You not only get things done, you want to excel and improve upon what has been done previously. You have the strength and energy to get where you want to go.

YOUR SUPERPOWERS:

Focus, Commitment, Positivity, Confidence

WEAKNESSES TO STRENGTHEN:

Faultfinding, Inflexibility, Arrogance, Negativity

YOUR MISSION FOR POWER:

Take time for consideration. You will be much more effective and dedicated in everything you do if you consider all options before jumping in. This will ensure your ultimate success.

Give yourself permission. You might feel that you need to spring into action and embrace change head on, but instead, you need to deliberate and acclimate to any changes. Give yourself time to contemplate.

Double-check as you go along. You work best when you feel safe and secure. If you move too quickly, you could develop a painful fear of failure.

Make a system to get yourself going. When working with others, start with a timeline and system so you can pour your heart into moving forward on track. You'll motivate others with your enthusiasm when you know how you'll get there.

Look forward to a positive outcome. When you are unsure, you tend to feel immobilized. Catalyze yourself to action by talking about and envisioning what you want to produce.

LIFE AFFIRMATION: "I trust that everything I need to get to where I want to go is on its way to me. I remain patient and focused on the next step."

When you first start out on any journey, what you need is not always available. However, have you noticed that once you begin, the right situation, person, circumstances, and opportunities seem to magically line up? It's no different with the challenges you may be facing right now. Don't overwhelm yourself and create stress by thinking too far ahead. Take it step by step. Make the best decision you can right now, based on what you know and *not* on what you fear will or will not happen, otherwise you'll drive yourself crazy. Use this affirmation to let the present be your master, not a fear-fabricated future in an incomplete and incorrect reality.

ENERGY-BALANCING ACTIVITIES: (Refer to Appendix A at the end of Part Two for ideas.)

When you feel emotional: Earth activities

When you feel mentally stressed: Metal activities

When you feel burnt-out: Water activities

When you feel stuck: Wood activities

When you feel uninspired: Fire activities

ALCOR TALITHA

Metal + Earth

The Masterful Ally

Aka: The Competent Helper and The Reserved Mediator

PRIMARY ELEMENT: Metal (Alcor)

SECONDARY ELEMENT: Earth (Talitha)

YOUR OVERVIEW: As a Masterful Ally, you are a strong supporter of any person, project, or cause to which you have committed, and you do what it takes to move things toward manifestation, even in the face of obstacles. Since personal glory is not your objective, you naturally take others into consideration in all you do. You like to accomplish what you feel responsible for, and you thrive when you are able to set a routine that can reduce risk. Your contemplative yet caring nature makes people feel safe with you.

You are a loyal source of energy, and you like to be well prepared. Even when things are chaotic, though, you maintain a steady demeanor and help everyone stay grounded. You delight in situations where everyone agrees. People are drawn to you as a Competent Helper for your dependability. As a Reserved Mediator, you are called upon as someone who can respond to problems and times of crisis with calm and careful reasoning.

YOUR PURPOSE: You are here to be a consistent and wisdom-filled presence for the people in your life who need to know that someone cares.

YOUR CREED: "I take my time so I can do it perfectly."

YOUR CORE DESIRE: To stay focused on your own goals and needs, yet still have time to help others.

YOUR CORE VALUE: To stay in control, to be caring, and to keep the peace.

AT YOUR BEST: You are kind, helpful, and considerate. You show others you care, yet you are able to hold your boundaries well and not over-give of your time and energy. You are reliable, do things efficiently, and are comfortable spending time alone in contemplation as well as with others that you care about.

AT YOUR WORST: You are picky, controlling, stubborn, and dismissive. You worry too much and overprepare unnecessarily. You internalize your anger and build up resentment over time because you don't communicate your feelings. You can get stuck in a rut for a very long time.

YOUR ARCHETYPE TWIN: Earth + Metal – Reliable Analyst

MOST COMPATIBLE WITH:

Water + Earth – Reflective Confidant

Earth + Water – Calm Connector

MOST SUPPORTED BY:

Fire + Earth – Energetic Protector

Earth + Fire – Loyal Cheerleader

MOST DRAINING FOR YOU:

Water + Metal – Caring Perfectionist

Metal + Water – Focused Visionary

YOUR GREATEST TEACHER:

Wood + Fire – Innovative Idealist

Fire + Wood – Spontaneous Initiator

YOUR ELEMENTAL DYNAMIC: Nurturing

Earth supports Metal and together they create sustainability, so when you are in balance, you are resilient and unshakeable. However, since Metal also uses up the nutrients from Earth, it's important to take time to nurture both elements and not depend on Earth to be the energy generator.

If too much emphasis is placed on Earth qualities (staying safe, being compassionate and conservative) and not enough on Metal qualities (being creative and open to change), which Metal thrives on, you suffer from stagnancy and lack of progress. If, however, you are over-controlling, you shut off the flow you need to attain your personal goals.

SUPPORTING ELEMENT: Fire

Fire supports the elements of Metal and Earth. In the elemental cycle, Fire produces Earth, which in turn cultivates Metal. Fire is the element that supports and connects Metal through Earth, so when you feel at odds with yourself, tired, or out of balance, it is extremely beneficial to being in Fire energy, which can be as simple as spending some time outdoors being active.

Having Fire elements in your environment is essential for support. Wall art depicting sunrises and all shades of the colors red, purple, and orange are considered beneficial for Metal/Earth Integrated Archetypes.

Fire energy is about freedom and movement, and being social and uninhibited, so it can be helpful to make a point of spending time with individuals who have Fire as a part of their makeup (e.g., Avior – Superhero Archetype Three) can be helpful.

YOUR PERSONAL VIRTUES:

Resilient: Your resilience is second to none. When there is a challenge or setback, you respond calmly and remain unfazed even when others are in chaos.

Dedicated: You are physically and mentally dedicated and are slow to tire.

Rational: You are methodical and can present your ideas with clarity. You are also careful and rational.

Subtle: You are understated and quietly do what you need to do without having the need to shine the spotlight on yourself. Your results speak for themselves.

Considerate: You are considerate in the midst of conflict. You know to point out facts objectively when emotion is present, yet also know the importance of making sure that everyone is heard.

YOUR SUPERPOWERS:

Focus, Commitment, Patience, Consideration

WEAKNESSES TO STRENGTHEN:

Faultfinding, Inflexibility, Procrastination, Resistance to change

YOUR MISSION FOR ACTION:

Learn about the goals of people you care about. You have the ability to help others be successful. When you nurture people by helping them get what they want in life, you are fulfilled.

Speak up when you have a better way. You tend to subordinate to others, but make sure you let them know when you see how something can be done better or more efficiently.

Think things through, but not too much. You have an analytical mind and want things to be perfect, but remember that you make progress when you let go.

Remember that you inspire trust in people. You are cautious and considerate about sensitive topics, and you handle delicate issues well. Because of this people are loyal to you.

Explain your decisions to others. You are conservative in your decision making, especially during times of change. Instead of keeping silent, let people know the advantages of your point of view.

LIFE AFFIRMATION: "I expand my thinking beyond what I believe is possible. I take my focus off the obstacles and look towards my vision."

What you believe you achieve. If you believe that you can only go so far in life, guess what? That's as far as you will go. It's good to remind yourself that you can do more than you think possible. That's because we human beings tend to see the impossibilities rather than the possibilities in a situation. And even when we do set goals, we still tend to focus on the challenges, setting ourselves up to be less and achieve much less than we are truly able to. Use this affirmation to remind yourself to think big and stay focused on what's possible.

ENERGY-BALANCING ACTIVITIES: (Refer to Appendix A at the end of Part Two for ideas.)

When you feel emotional: Earth activities

When you feel mentally stressed: Metal activities

When you feel burnt-out: Water activities

When you feel stuck: Wood activities

When you feel uninspired: Fire activities

PART TWO

APPENDIX

ELEMENTAL ENERGY BALANCING ACTIVITIES

WATER: Nourish yourself with Water by going swimming or taking a long, relaxing bath. Spend time at a spa or a steam room, or hang out in a Jacuzzi. Get lost in a book, movie, or story. Meditate with music. Walk along the beach near the edge of the water. Schedule some downtime to "do nothing," or do something you've been missing but have been putting off. Take a Tai Chi or Chi Kung class. Have a deep conversation with a trusted friend or a heart-to-heart with someone who really understands you.

WOOD: Get your body moving by going for a light jog or a speed walk around the block. Take a yoga class or do some stretching exercises. Make time to organize your environment: pick a drawer, cabinet, or shelf and neaten it up. Open your calendar and make plans for the upcoming day, week, or month. Visually lay out your schedule so you can see something tangible and organized. Make decisions now that might save you time later. Have a stimulating conversation or a fun debate with a friend or watch a comedy show.

FIRE: Get a bunch of friends together and do something fun and spontaneous. Spend time socializing or going to where the people and action are. Attend a live performance or event or watch an action-packed movie at the theater. Do something impulsive and spontaneous and go where your heart leads you. Eat spicy food. Go shopping. Go dancing. Talk to someone you love hanging out with and make plans to travel or do something fun. Take a high-energy exercise class like Zumba, MMA Kickboxing, or Bootcamp. Hang out in bright, open spaces.

EARTH: Walk in nature, visit with a close friend, cook, draw, paint—something creative. Get a massage. Do aromatherapy. Set some achievable goals for the week. Go to the health-food store and buy food that is healthy and nourishing. Complete a project that you've been stalling on. Give yourself permission to do "nothing" but watch TV, read, or be a couch potato at home. Spend time with the family members you like. Spend quality time with your pet. Offer to help someone with a task or project. Practice a craft. Stay home and light candles. Wear your oldest most comfortable house clothes and turn off your cell phone and social media notifications.

METAL: Do something you're really good at doing, something you've already mastered, so you can feel accomplished. Pick a location in your house—perhaps your room, desk, or car—and clear and clean it as best you can. Polish all the metal or shiny surfaces in your house to take off water marks and make the shiny surfaces shiny again. Talk to someone who is analytical. Spend time alone. Do something that requires you to work out logistics. Neaten up your computer desktop. Clear digital clutter. Clear physical clutter from your desk or a small area you frequent often. Clear off all countertops in your home.

PART THREE

NEUTRALIZE YOUR WEAKNESSES

CHAPTER 5

What is Your Weakness?

Anger	Faultfinding	People Pleasing
Anxiety	Fear	Overwhelm
Arrogance	Guilt	Procrastination
Blaming	Impatience	Resentment
Defensiveness	Inability to Say No	Self-Doubt
Distraction	Indecisiveness	Stress
Emotional Dependency	Insecurity	Stubbornness
Faultfinding	Low Self-Esteem	Vanity
Fear	Negative Thinking	Worry

We have all met our powerlessness and we have all faced our weaknesses in one way or another in our lives. Most of us will admit we have aspects of ourselves that if improved upon would make our lives easier, and help ourselves to be more confident and powerful. Yet, it's not easy to put forth effort towards improvement when there is no reason to. As well, it's often easier to use our weaknesses as an excuse - "It's just the way that I am. I'm an impatient person. I can't help it."

If we all had magical powers, we could snap our fingers and have patience, resilience, persistence and whatever we need show up when we are in the midst of our challenges. In the case of being human, it's not that easy, and we must either go through life experiences to gain our strength, or use conscious awareness coupled with intent to master the next level of who we are.

To transcend weaknesses that inhibit us and to reach balance in our lives, most important is to embrace the fact that every moment of every day, you have a choice. Even though there will be conflict and obstacles that test your powers and emphasize your weaknesses, if you prepare, you can find power. By consciously bettering ourselves, we evolve our wisdom and our lives to the next level.

If you want to keep on getting what you are getting in your life, then the answer is to keep on doing exactly what you are doing. If you want to taste the delight of life when you are in control and in power, then do something different. Like a superhero, make different choices in the moment. The wisdom you gain will carry you powerfully through every stage of your life.

WEAKNESSES TO MINIMIZE

ANGER

Associated Archetypes: Although everyone gets angry at times, if you have Fire (Avior), Wood (Nexus), or Metal (Alcor) as a primary or secondary archetype, you may relate to anger as a specific weakness.

What: We all know what anger is, and we have all felt it. It is completely normal to feel angry; anger is a naturally occurring human emotion. It can help you stand up for yourself and others as you affirm to yourself that what you feel is right. Only when anger gets out of control or turns destructive is it time to reassess. If you can harness the emotional aspects of anger and not be at the mercy of it, you move into power.

Awareness to Embrace: *Shoulds* may be the ultimate source of your anger.

Many of us think that other people's behavior causes our anger—that someone is doing something that irritates you and makes you angry. Why is it, then, that not everyone else is getting angry, too? There is no single behavior that consistently angers every one of us all of the time. When you feel angry about something, it is because you have *shoulds* associated with it. External occurrences on their own are not what make you angry; you get angry because of how you assess those occurrences. You get angry because you frame the behavior as wrong and then expect that others should follow your assessment.

Mission to Power:

1. Become less judgmental.

Since anger is driven by how you think and feel others *should* behave, it is a highly egotistical emotion when out of control. The key is to see the various rules you've been living by for what they are. Was anger a big part of the way you were brought up? Is it just your way of doing things? Isn't it crazy to judge others for not following your rules?

It is helpful to remind yourself of the countless ways in which human beings operate. Not everyone does the same things the same way. There will always be someone to agree with you and someone to disagree with you.

Having opinions is fine, but if you are convinced that your way is the only way, that your way is right and universal, you will feel restricted and express yourself through anger.

2. Explain, don't blame. Think logically.

When we are angry, we say things like he *should* or *shouldn't* have done this or that because "it made me angry." Instead, look at others' behavior differently. Don't condemn it. Explain it to yourself. For example, "For him to have acted that way means that he must have a different brain and different beliefs." Focus on what caused the behavior. Did the person have a different kind of upbringing? Is she from a different culture? Behavior is complex and involves many variables, but the key is to practice moving away from blame and take responsibility by opening your mind to new ways of thinking. Once you can see some possible causes for a behavior, your anger will lessen naturally.

3. Show empathy.

Empathy is intuitive. It's about "living in the skin" of another person. Empathy is a great antidote to anger because it's hard to be mad at someone if you really understand where they are coming from. When we are angry, we are unable to understand it. That's why we say things like: "Why would you do that?" "What's wrong with you?" "How could you do something like that?"

As you work to diminish your anger, turn these questions on yourself. Asking them of yourself helps to turn your focus away from blame so that you can work on understanding another person's perspective, and that will strengthen you.

Affirmations for Strength:

- I choose to be present and aware in every moment.

- I notice and accept differences in opinion everywhere I look.

- My stumbling blocks become my stepping stones to new opportunities.

ANXIETY

Associated Archetypes: All archetypes experience anxiety as part of their elemental temperament when feeling less than confident in who they are and when striving for perfection in their own way.

What: Anxiety is apprehension about something in the future about which we both consciously and unconsciously predict bad, scary outcomes that do not have any basis in truth. This causes physical and emotional discomfort and makes you unable to enjoy the present because your mind is racing back and forth among undesirable, bad, and painful outcomes.

Awareness to Embrace: Anxiety has been proven to be reversed with regular focus on relaxation techniques.

While anxiety can be more present in those who have a predisposition to it due to genetics or due to experiences in the womb or growing up, a study at Harvard Medical School demonstrated that even deep-rooted tendencies toward anxiety can be physiologically and even anatomically reversed with regular focus.

Relaxation techniques actually change the architecture of an anxious brain by shrinking the fear area and strengthening the rational area.

Mission to Power:

1. Accept that you have anxiety.

Instead of wishing it would go away or that you didn't have it, accept it by remembering that anxiety is just a feeling like any other feeling. It's simply an emotional reaction. Just as happiness is an emotional reaction to seeing someone you love, anxiety is an emotional reaction to fearing that you will get something you don't love.

The first step to power is to accept the anxiety, because the more you resist it, the worse it gets; resistance perpetuates the thought that your anxiety is unbearable. Accepting it doesn't mean that you like it; it means that you are open to the benefit of accepting the reality that it exists within you. In other words, you are not trying to get rid of it in the moment, you are accepting that it is part of the moment.

2. Realize that your brain is playing tricks on you—even lying!

When anxiety is present, it feels very real. This is because the scenarios that your brain creates for you would be extremely challenging—if they were real. Regularly take a moment to go to the source of your anxiety and remind yourself that what you are envisioning *isn't real*. Doing this will begin to create a new pattern of awareness and a habit of not believing every vision and every thought that provokes fear. This is a process of taking charge. Do not believe every thought that is creating your anxiety. (See "Worry" for related information.)

3. Induce your body's relaxation response regularly.

One of the best ways to defend against anxiety is to induce the body's relaxation response and do it regularly. This concept was first introduced by Harvard researcher Dr. Herbert Benson, and it has shown to decrease muscle tension, slow heart rate, decrease blood pressure, and lower the levels of stress hormones in the body. Do this daily:

Ten minutes in the morning: Use a relaxation technique that resonates with you. It might be listening to soothing nature sounds; it might be breathing deeply; it might be consciously scanning your body and relaxing each body part; it might be listening to a guided visualization, focusing on the words of calming affirmations; or it might be a combination of these.

Throughout the day: Bring consciousness to your breathing throughout the day, and do it intentionally when you feel stressed. When we are stressed, we tend to breath shallowly; and when we are anxious, we feel worse when not well oxygenated. Shallow breathing also contributes to muscle tension.

Use the 4-6-8 breathing technique: Breathe in through your nose for 4 counts, hold your breath deep in your lungs for 6 counts, and then slowly breathe out through your mouth for 8 counts. Do a few rounds of this whenever you can—when you are driving, when you're on hold on the phone, or even in between work tasks.

4. For specific problems, create a focused time to think about them.

We've all gone through times when we couldn't stop thinking about a certain undesirable outcome. For example, let's say you are waiting on results from a health test that provokes a lot of anxiety about the future, or that you are in the midst of a law suit and don't know if it will work out in your favor. In cases like this, worrying around the clock is natural, given that your life might go through a big change, but all this worrying and the levels of stress it induces is not good for your health.

In such a case, set aside a designated time each day to think about or write about your concerns and feelings. Write out the worst-case scenarios and then strategize as to what you would do should the worst happen. When you start obsessing outside this designated time, stop and remind yourself that you'll spend time on it during the next designated time.

Affirmations for Strength:

- I trust in the divine workings of the Universe and recognize that there is always a bigger picture to consider that supports me in every way.

- I am the master of multiple realities, and I see the advantageous outcome in every situation.

- I look for synchronicities to affirm that I am on the right path and that everything is going to be all right.

ARROGANCE

Associated Archetypes: If you have Fire (Avior), Wood (Nexus), or Metal (Alcor) as a primary or secondary archetype, you may relate to having arrogance as a weakness.

What: While no one likes to think that they are arrogant, some archetypes are more prone to it than others. Arrogance is having or showing an attitude to others that you think you are better, smarter, or more important. While confidence inspires others and lets people know who you are, arrogance turns people off. When you become over-confident, exaggerate your abilities, and see yourself as above others, you set yourself up for over-confidence and ignorance.

Awareness to Embrace: A thin line exists between feeling confident and believing you are above others.

There is something called "authentic pride," in which you feel confident, productive, and good about who you are. When your ego and arrogance take over, that's called "hubristic pride." If you tend to tune out when others want to share their knowledge with you, or if at times you notice you're thinking that other people's opinions are worthless, then you will have caught yourself in a state of arrogance.

Mission to Power:

1. Increase your self-awareness.

By being self-aware, you can avoid falling into the arrogance trap. It feels good to be arrogant because you are putting yourself above others, but there is nothing more inspiring than someone who is confident and also humble. Here are some questions to ask yourself:

- Do you interrupt people so you can share what you think?
- Do you offer advice even when not called upon?
- Do you blame others when things go wrong?
- When others don't share your same viewpoint, do you dismiss them?

2. Admit your errors.

Own your actions. Accept that you mess up. Be accountable for your mistakes. Once you see that you make mistakes, too, it frees you from having to pretend that you are better than anyone else. Our ego wants to win at all costs, but to stay humble, it is important to admit your shortfalls.

3. Remind yourself often that there are other truths.

There is more than one truth, and more than one way to do things. There are many answers and many viewpoints. It is okay to be wrong. It is okay to accept that there may be answers other than yours. Life is a journey of discovery, and new truths continue to emerge. We don't know enough to know everything there is to know, so it's wise to remain open.

Affirmations for Strength:

- I am open to expanding my sphere of influence and wisdom.
- I give myself permission to be open to new ways of seeing and doing things.
- Everything I experience is an experience based in love and humility.

BLAMING

Associated Archetypes: If you have Fire (Avior), Wood (Nexus), or Metal (Alcor) as a primary or secondary archetype, you may relate to having an issue with blame.

What: Blame is holding someone or something else responsible for whatever has gone wrong. The ego defends itself by blaming others. We deny that we are wrong because we think it protects us from looking bad or being punished. We don't want to be at fault, so when we are confronted with an uncomfortable truth, we all have a tendency to move in the direction of blame. Unfortunately, people see right through it.

Awareness to Embrace: When you take responsibility for your actions, you enter the zone of positivity.

Blaming others is convenient, but doing anything other than taking responsibility will never uplift you. It puts you in the role of victim. Here's a great wisdom to embrace: Affirm, "Nothing happens *to* me; everything happens *for* me." Next time you are inclined to blame someone, ask yourself, "How did this happen *for* me?" Or, "How am I benefitting in this situation?" These questions will unstick you from an old pattern of powerlessness and negativity.

When you look for how an unfortunate situation is helping you, you're not giving your power to someone else (by letting them get you in an emotional state), and you will be able to use the situation to enter the "zone of positivity." When you blame, you enter a negative zone, and consequently, you attract more negative thoughts and stay small. Finding the benefit and the opportunity in the moment is not easy during a challenge, but it ultimately empowers you to grow.

Mission to Power:

1. Become aware of when you are formulating an excuse.

If it's a habit for you to jump to blame or excuses, the first step is to objectively observe your ego scrambling for an excuse or for someone or something else to blame. You can do this not only when you are confronted by a person or situation, but also when you see that things are not going as you want.

2. Start getting comfortable with owning everything.

Make the decision to own everything in your life, both big and small things, and your life will move toward a simpler path. You don't have to make excuses or tell stories about why things are the way they are. You don't need to get defensive anymore, or try to prove yourself right. You are giving yourself a gift in the form of freedom. Your self-respect builds, and you'll be able to see yourself, and in turn others, more clearly.

3. Focus on what's ahead and how to make things better.

Once you decide, "Okay, I'm taking responsibility," then it is wisest to move on and put your focus on how to improve. Accepting responsibility for what goes wrong means you can also accept credit for what goes right. You have the ability to affect your life and its direction, no matter what happens.

Affirmations for Strength:

- I am responsible for everything in my life, including my thoughts, my words, and my actions.
- My mistakes are my stepping-stones to new opportunities.
- I have the power to manifest, direct, and create the life of my dreams.

DEFENSIVENESS

Associated Archetypes: If you have Water (Selene), Wood (Nexus), or Metal (Alcor) as a primary or secondary archetype, you may relate to having an issue with getting defensive when you are criticized.

What: Defensiveness is an unconscious and automatic response to perceived danger. It's natural get defensive when you think you are being criticized or accused of being somehow inadequate. It's a response to the basic need to protect yourself. If you grew up being put down a lot or were regularly criticized, you might have become allergic to any statement or request that can be interpreted as suggesting inadequacy of any kind.

Awareness to Embrace: You needed to protect yourself with defensiveness in the past, but you no longer have to do that.

If you've developed defensiveness as an instinctive protective shield, innocent statements and questions may feel like attacks, even if they are not. If you've ever been told that you are oversensitive, or if you know that you tend to take things the wrong way, know that you can change your outdated behavior with intention, willingness, and a plan. You can respond to others in the future with knowledge of your worthiness and learn to trust that you are being treated with care and respect.

Mission to Power:

1. Start paying attention to what happens when you get defensive.

Notice how you respond when someone gets your defenses up. Does your body get tense? Do you feel like you need to justify yourself or your behavior? What is the topic under discussion? Your behavior? Your looks? Your success? Your status? The way you spend money? Pay attention to the topic and your response. Don't judge yourself, just notice.

2. Acknowledge what is happening.

Once you notice your response, before you "retaliate" and react in the normal way, take a few deep breaths to slow things down. Say to yourself, "I'm feeling defensive. Let me take a moment and hear what is actually being said." For example, let's say your spouse says, "Is that a new shirt?" and, immediately, you think it is an insinuation that you are wasting money. You want to retort, "I work hard. I deserve it." Or maybe you feel the need to justify the purchase: "It was on sale. It was only twenty dollars." What if all you really need to say is, "Yes, it's new. I like the color, and it was the right price." Or maybe it's even simpler than that. Maybe all you need to say is, "Yes. Yes, it is."

3. Ask a question to build the conversation positively.

Build on what the person says to buy time to realize that you are not being attacked. Let's say you are asked, "Why didn't you do more on that project?" Instead of reacting defensively, say something like, "Tell me more about what you mean." Or, "What are some ideas you have about that?" This gives you time to see where the person is coming from. It's possible they are simply curious, not cutting you down.

Affirmations for Strength:

- I respond to those I speak to daily with balance, grace, and ease.
- I have the right words to say, and I say them in just the right way.
- I am the master of my reality, and I choose to see my reality in the way that serves me and others best.

DISTRACTION

Associated Archetypes: If you have Wood (Nexus) or Fire (Avior) as a primary or secondary archetype, you may relate to having an issue with distraction.

What: Distraction can take many forms, and the concept itself is difficult to define. Distraction can be internal (thoughts, desires, hunger, emotions, etc.) or external (internet, irritations, interruptions, sounds, etc.). It can be habitual, uncontrollable, annoying, or even welcome. Actually, distraction can be useful to give us a break from something we are trying to escape. Distraction is caused by an inability to pay attention, by a lack of interest in the object of attention, or by the novelty of something other than the object of attention that interferes with focus.

Awareness to Embrace: You will allow distraction to refocus you from anything you want to escape.

Children don't get distracted when playing video games, but they do when they've been told to do their homework. You don't get distracted when you are engrossed in something that has captured your full attention, but you do when you are working on a must-do project. Yes, even though we now live in a world where there is ever more to distract us, we only get distracted when we don't really want to do what we think we *should* be doing. The downside is, the more we allow ourselves to get distracted, the easier it becomes to get distracted. This can affect our productivity and our ability to do what we need to do.

Distraction is inevitable. Yet, it's important to stay aware. If you are too distracted on an everyday basis, it may be wise to refocus on a new life goal or direction. Meanwhile, there are many techniques and strategies we can implement daily to minimize distractions. Will power is *not* the key to being able to focus. The key is to minimize distractions.

Mission to Power:

1. Define and understand your form of distraction.

Is it noise, emails, tech notifications, friends, interruptions, social media, a messy desk, TV, needing something new, internet, phone, fatigue, hunger, stress, smoking, spacing out, pain, need for pleasure, daily news, finding excitement, negative thoughts, anxiety, fear, worry, exhaustion, boredom, uncertainty, dread? When and where does it tend to happen? Why do you think it happens? Being clear on its form, location, and timing makes a big difference because now you know what to do.

2. Determine the type of distraction it is, and assess how much control you have over it.

- Is it a physical distraction: telephone ringing, friend stopping by, email pop-ups, social media notifications, clutter, messy desk? What percentage is in your control?

- Is it a physiological distraction: hunger, sleep deprivation, stress, pain, sickness, need for sex? What percentage is in your control?

- Is it a cognitive distraction: a song stuck in your head, negative thoughts, a stressful situation, too much on your mind, worry? What percentage is in your control?

3. Create specific plans to make focus easier.

We are hard-wired to pay attention to distractions, so by minimizing them, you increase your ability to focus. Will you, for example, only answer emails during set hours? Clear your desk off before working? Turn off your social media notifications? Let people know that you are not available during a certain period of time? If you have specific physiological or cognitive distractions, look for what you can do to minimize their effect on your focus.

4. Start each day with a distraction-freeing ritual.

As an example: Each morning, clear off your desk, disable tech distractions, put on headphones, put your phone and tablet on silent (preferably in another location far from reach), get something to drink, and set an intention for what you plan to accomplish. After an hour, give yourself ten to fifteen minutes to do whatever you like—check emails, take a walk, look at your phone, etc.

5. Plan ahead by letting sleep do the work for you.

Research has found that our brain goes over our day when we are sleeping and creates memories for us. It transfers the day's information from short-term memory to long-term and organizes our thoughts. Whatever we plan at night, we can use to work for us the next day.

As you lie in bed before you fall asleep, tell yourself what tomorrow looks like. As an example, if you decide to start each day with a distraction-freeing ritual, as mentioned above, go over that sequence in your head. When you are asleep, the pattern of thought will be set, and you will be much more likely to follow the plan and not get distracted.

Affirmations for Strength:

- I am here on earth to inspire and be inspired and to give myself permission to be the master of my life.

- My goal today is to be present in every moment.

- I decide where I want to play in the game of life, and I focus on what brings me closer to my success.

EMOTIONAL DEPENDENCY

Associated Archetypes: If you have Water (Selene) or Earth (Talitha) as a primary or secondary archetype, you may relate to having a tendency towards dependency.

What: Dependency can take many forms, but the central theme is seeking a sense of fulfillment from something or someone external to you. Usually, it's love, security, approval, or value from another. For example, you might feel that you "need" a partner to feel secure or complete, or that you "need" a prestigious job title to feel important. Food, alcohol, money, social media "likes," work, or even our cell phones can serve as objects for our emotional dependency.

Awareness to Embrace: When your fulfillment depends on something outside yourself, know that it is possible to develop less attachment.

Yes, it's important to have others in your life with whom to share love and feel support. But when you are overly dependent on something outside yourself, you feel insecure and fearful; you think that without it, you don't have what it takes to be whole. Dependency arises when you minimize the importance or value of your time, your existence, or your energy.

If you have difficulty disagreeing with others, feel that you are responsible when bad things happen, think you have to fulfill others' expectations, need outside validation for what you do or who you are, or have a hard time holding personal boundaries, you have some degree of dependency on what others think, giving you the need for outside validation.

The more dependent you are, the more important it is to work towards your independence. Use your dependent traits to guide you towards finding out what lies on the other side of your insecurity or fear so that you can move towards more self-fulfillment.

Mission to Power:

1. Set an intent to redefine the relationship you have with what you depend on.

When you depend on something (being liked, being needed, being important, being thought of as "nice," being in control, etc.), it's because your mind has become deeply attached to it. Your relationship to that person, concept, or object is one of intense involvement, making it hard to disengage because it's something that you are conditioned to desire and think you need. The first step is to decide that you want to detach. This means deciding that becoming more independent is the focus of your current journey. You must commit to it for the long haul, as it will take some diligence and practice to move towards freedom.

2. Ask yourself what exactly you need, and then prioritize that need.

When you become aware that you are needy, instead of telling yourself, "I wish I wasn't like this," or "I wish I could let go," think about taking a new direction. Use your need as a path to pursue. Your needs won't go away if you neglect or ignore them, so write them down. What is it you need? Is it approval, praise, to be liked, to feel important, to be included, to be accepted? The key is this: you need to start doing more for yourself. Part of looking after yourself is to figure out not only what you need, but also how to help yourself get it. Make that your priority, and search out resources.

3. Schedule intentional self-time and practice savoring it.

As children, we learn how to become emotionally independent by the simple act of playing. Think of self-time as "play time," and give yourself the opportunity to rediscover the joy of spontaneity. Make time to look after yourself, and intentionally do things for yourself. Start small if you're not used to it. There are many ways to begin. You might begin by learning how to breathe calmly. Pick up a new hobby, learn meditation, go for regular walks, regularly treat yourself to something you like. Transform the experience of being with yourself, and you will become your own best friend for life.

Affirmations for Strength:
- I have everything within me to fulfill myself, my life, and my dreams.
- I spend time with myself and learn more about myself each day.
- I decide where I want to play in the game of life. I give myself permission to be the master of my own life.

FAULTFINDING

Associated Archetypes: If you have Fire (Avior), Wood (Nexus), or Metal (Alcor) as a primary or secondary archetype, you may relate to having an issue with being critical and judgmental.

What: Most of us do not realize how much and how often we judge and criticize others. We gossip about people, look down on the way they do things we think we do better—the list goes on and on. When we criticize someone, it says nothing about that person; really, it only says something about our own need to be critical. Having opinions is one thing, but to look at another's actions or inactions and criticize them is inferring that you are superior to them.

Awareness to Embrace: When you are critical of others, you are actually being critical of yourself.

We love to compare ourselves favorably with those around us. When our ego takes the lead, and we come out ahead, we feel good. Notice where you are most critical? These are the areas in which you feel vulnerable, not good enough. If you are constantly worried about being a good leader, you might be quicker to look down on someone who doesn't lead well. When you roll your eyes on hearing that someone missed a deadline again, it's because you're still beating yourself up for flaking out on deadlines. This comparison is not conscious. Being critical of others makes you feel, "At least I'm better than that."

While it may feel good to point out how others are screwing up, judgment extinguishes empathy, and empathy is needed for trust, intimacy, and all things loving. It's impossible to be understanding toward others when we are criticizing them.

Mission to Power:

1. Figure out the circumstances in which you tend to judge.

There are three circumstances in which people tend to be critical.

- When you see someone exhibiting the same objectionable behavior as you, but you pretend you don't or don't realize that you do. For example, you may criticize someone for always being late even though you also are often late, although you pretend you aren't and that, when you are, it's for a good reason.

- When someone breaks a rule that you secretly want to break but don't allow yourself. In the same example above, you wish you could disregard protocol and not worry about inconveniencing others, but you don't let yourself.

- When you hold a belief in your value system that says a specific behavior is immoral. In the same example above, you may have been taught by your parents that being late is a sign of extreme disrespect.

2. Embrace your own imperfections.

Start with being kind to yourself. Express compassion for yourself. You need to feel comfortable with your own choices and able to embrace your own imperfections before you can stop feeling the need to criticize and judge others. Remember, whenever you judge or criticize another, you are really being hard on yourself.

3. Be mindful by staying aware of your thoughts, feelings, and words.

Embrace mindfulness, which is the seed that nurtures change. Be awake to what you are thinking about others, and what you are saying. How does it feel when you are being critical? Most important, ask why you are being critical. It might seem awkward at first, but next time you feel judgmental, ask yourself, "What is really going on here? It's not about her; it's about me." Judgment and criticism of others is always a reference to the self.

Affirmations for Strength:

- I accept myself as I am, and by doing so, I accept others for who they are.
- I see the presence of love everywhere I look.
- I give myself permission to be who I am.

FEAR

Associated Archetypes: Although every archetype certainly experiences fear, if you have Water (Selene) or Wood (Nexus) as a primary or secondary archetype, you may relate to having an issue with fear.

What: Fear can take many forms, but at its core, it's an uncomfortable emotional response to a threat, and not only to a real threat, but also to a perceived threat. For example, we can fear a potential outcome although there might not be any real danger.

Fear keeps us alive. It's the warning mechanism for avoiding something that might cause us harm. When we make life choices, fear cautions us by making us feel frightened to take chances, even if the outcome could be advantageous. When experiencing fear, we act on how we feel, and in many cases, we've created distorted and negative interpretations of all potential outcomes. Then, constantly thinking about a perceived negative outcome turns into anxiety and fear.

Awareness to Embrace: You can never get rid of fear, and avoiding the fear makes it worse.

As a natural defense mechanism, fear's "job" is to alert you to possible dangers, however, avoiding what you are afraid of will only make you more afraid. We've all heard the phrase, "Face your fears," and it is good advice. This is due to "habituation," the mechanism whereby familiar things get boring over time. We are hard-wired to habituate to what is familiar—and that includes fear. By avoiding what causes your fear, you keep the fear with you because your nervous system can't find relief.

For example, if you have a fear about public speaking and avoid all situations which require you to do so, over time you'll live in a prison of avoidance when it comes to public speaking. Avoidance eliminates exposure, and avoiding the anxiety-provoking situation not only maintains it, but magnifies it.

Mission to Power:

1. Expose yourself to the fear.

Capitalize on the principle of habituation by exposing yourself regularly to what is causing you fear or anxiety. Your short-term discomfort will lead to a way out. Exposure to the fear is scary; we expect the fear to keep rising indefinitely.

However, any fear, if you face it, will subside as you habituate. Exposure works much better than avoidance because it is the physiological antidote to anxiety.

Confronting your fear brings a sense of accomplishment. Every time you consciously expose yourself to that which you fear (meeting new people, giving a speech, saying no, speaking up, etc.), your anxiety is losing strength while you are gaining power. What we fear is not the actual object or activity; we fear the sensations of fear.

2. Remind yourself that, realistically, what you fear will not kill you.

Consciously ask yourself questions such as:

- Is this worry realistic?
- What would be the worst possible outcome?
- Am I exaggerating the outcome?
- Is what I am afraid of the worst possible outcome?
- If that happens, can I handle it?
- What are a few positive outcomes that I'm forgetting are possible?
- What can I do to prepare for the worst?

3. Use visualization to create ease.

Practice the following meditation regularly so that you will be able to access it the moment you feel fear or anxiety. As you do the visualization, do not label your feelings as good or bad; simply acknowledge that they exist and let them pass by.

Envision yourself in nature. You're lying comfortably on the grass or on the beach, gazing at the sky. Assign your thoughts, sensations, and emotions to the clouds and watch them float away.

Affirmations for Strength:

- I will not veer from my desire to find peace, even if I face hurdles along the way.
- My stumbling blocks become my stepping-stones to new opportunities.
- I choose to find the most valuable reality in every situation.

GUILT

Associated Archetypes: If you have Water (Selene) or Earth (Talitha) as a primary or secondary archetype, you may relate to a tendency to feel guilty.

What: Guilt is like an inner watchdog that makes us feel bad if we don't do what we think we *should* do. Many people have difficulty letting go of their everyday guilt, such as financial guilt, feeling guilty when you spend money on something you think you *shouldn't;* friend and family guilt when you avoid them and feel bad; or kid guilt, when you do something for yourself instead of for them.

Guilt is an emotion that arises when you assume—unrealistically—that you have done something you think is "bad." The guilt is due to your judgment and your perception. As well, guilt can be helpful when it prompts you to rethink and realign your actions. However, often people make life excessively hard for themselves by holding onto a stubborn perspective that creates unnecessary guilt and stress.

Awareness to Embrace: If you change your perception of what you feel guilty about, your guilt will go away.

One way to deal with your guilt is to stack up all the *benefits* of the actions you are taking (or not taking) that are making you feel guilty. This will change your perception. If you can see that every event or action has both a positive and a "negative" side, you will neutralize your guilt and restore your balance. If you don't make the effort to uncover a different aspect, you will continue to suffer unnecessarily.

Mission to Power:

1. Let go of financial guilt.

Do you feel guilty if you buy something frivolous for yourself, get a beauty treatment that is not strictly necessary (such as a pedicure), pay more for something for convenience sake, or think you "waste money" by eating out all the time?

Here is a good reminder: money is a form of energy. Sometimes, we think of spending money as a "loss," failing to remember that the energy of the money is merely changing form. When you feel financial guilt coming on, ask yourself how the energy has changed form and in what way you have benefited. Do you feel better? If so, how did spending the money improve your mood? Boost your spirit? Save you energy? Look for the hidden benefit.

2. Let go of friend and family guilt.

Do you feel guilty if you see someone you know but purposely avoid them? Get a birthday present from someone when you didn't give one? Secretly dislike certain members of your family? If so, here is a reminder: whatever you want, feel, or do is okay. You experience guilt only when you judge that what you are feeling is bad. There is nothing wrong with valuing your time and energy enough that you avoid a potentially unpleasant situation. There are two sides to everything. Listen carefully to yourself and what you want without judging it.

You can't please everyone, and deep down, it never feels good when you betray yourself for the sake of pleasing another. As well, it is unrealistic to think that you will like everyone in this world, family or not. Choose to be self-centered, not in an it's-all-about-me way, but realistically.

3. Let go of guilt trips put on you by others.

Has someone ever said something that left you feeling guilty? For example, your family might make you feel guilty for not getting together more. This happens when we allow others to set the standard for what is "right," and whenever we don't follow their agenda, we feel bad.

The best way to handle this is to affirm that you can't please everyone, and everyone is responsible for themselves. It is not your "job" to do what others want you to do, no matter who they are.

4. Let go of kid guilt.

Do you feel guilty if you take a yoga class instead of taking your child somewhere they want to go? If you buy fast food for dinner? If you miss an important event for your child because you have to work? If you let your child play video games so that you can get some peace?

If these sound familiar, remind yourself that you are important, too. Sometimes, parents get lost in thinking that being "good" parents means sacrificing themselves, when, in fact, they simply need to know their priorities. When you live by what you see as a priority, your children may not get what they want in the short term, but they are getting what you see as the overall best, whether that means you making more money, doing something that makes you happier (therefore making you a happier parent), or doing something that saves time.

5. Let go of free-floating guilt.

Do you feel guilty if you mindlessly surf the Internet instead of doing something important? Eat a pint of ice cream before bed? Don't exercise as often as you should? Fantasize about having a different life even though you love your family?

If so, choose to be your own best supporter and limit your negative self-talk. Imagine your friend telling you that she feels guilty for the exact same thing. What would you say? It's likely that you would talk her out of feeling guilty. We all tend to judge ourselves too harshly.

Next time you feel guilty about something, tell yourself what you would tell a friend. Find some benefits to balance out the drawbacks. What did you gain? More time? More energy? A mental break? Remind yourself that judging what you did is worse than what you actually did.

Affirmations for Strength:

- Everything I am doing or not doing is serving a positive purpose.
- How I see things is in my mind and in my control.
- I focus on my own life and allow others to do the same.

IMPATIENCE

Associated Archetypes: If you have Fire (Avior) or Wood (Nexus) as a primary or secondary archetype, you may relate to having an issue with impatience.

What: Impatience arises when you seem to lack the capacity to accept or tolerate delay, difficulty, or annoyance without getting angry or upset. Your impatience has a cause, or often, a trigger. That could be a person, a phrase, or a specific situation (like traffic) that regularly causes you to enter an impatient state of mind. Impatience can cause you to experience one or more of the following: shallow breathing, muscle tension, anger, irritability, nervousness, anxiety, and the need to rush or verbally snap at others.

Awareness to Embrace: Everything happens at exactly the right time.

Sometimes we feel that things need to happen at the exact time and in the exact way that we want, and that the world and others should conform to our timing. It's wise to remember, however, that there is such a thing as "divine timing." Everything will happen exactly when it needs to. When you look back on your life, you can likely see that this is true. When we set up unrealistic expectations of the world and of ourselves and others, we set ourselves up to experience the uncomfortable emotion of impatience.

Mission to Power:

1. Take note when you are feeling impatient.

When things aren't going our way, we tend to think it's because of something external. But really, the cause is what's going on in your head about the situation. The best way to begin developing patience is to set the intention to alert yourself when you feel impatience arising in your mind as a response to not getting what you want right away.

2. Identify your triggers.

It's important to know what triggers you. Is it waiting in line? Trying to figure out how to fix something you are not familiar with? Someone who keeps you waiting? Listening to someone wax on and on about something simple? The main thing is to notice how impatience arises when you are not getting your way, even though you know you don't have direct control over the situation.

Usually impatience shows up in one of these categories of expectation. In which category are you most unrealistic?

- Wanting the environment to conform to you (e.g., traffic)

- Wanting people to conform to you (e.g., show up on time)

- Wanting to master things faster (e.g., I *should* be smarter or more capable).

3. Patiently redirect your thoughts and transform through mindfulness.

When you notice that you are getting impatient, such as when you are stuck in traffic or when someone in front of you is taking a long time, note the feeling in your body and mind. Ask yourself if there is anything you can do to change the situation. Usually, there isn't, so this is where mindfulness comes in.

Take a few deep breaths. Then, make a conscious effort to refocus and relax your muscles. Instead of focusing on the traffic or the irritating person in front of you, focus on something else. If in traffic, find a song you like on the radio, call someone, use the time to think about a solution to a problem, or plan the next day's meal. If you're in line, be curious about what else is going on. You have two choices: one is to be upset and irritated; the other is to find a way to make the experience more pleasant.

We often have unrealistic expectations about mastering new skills. If you're trying to fix your computer or assemble some shelves and are getting impatient with yourself, this is where you can consciously slow down and incorporate more kindness into your self-expectations. Make it a point to focus on enjoying the process. Commend yourself for doing what you are doing instead of focusing on getting it done faster.

Affirmations for Strength:

- I have realistic expectations of myself and others.

- I embrace divine timing and recognize that everything happens at exactly the right time, in exactly the right way.

- My goal today is to be present in every moment, and every experience I have is designed for my growth and evolution.

INABILITY TO SAY NO

Associated Archetypes: If you have Water (Selene) or Earth (Talitha) as a primary or secondary archetype, you may have a hard time saying no.

What: Some people find it hard to say no. There are a few basic reasons for this. It could be that you are a helper by nature and think you should help even if it eats into your personal time. Or, maybe you don't want to be thought of as rude—you want to be seen as agreeable. Or, you want to avoid conflict and not put yourself in an unpleasant situation. Sometimes, it's hard to say no because you want to maintain a relationship. Perhaps you don't value your time and think you should give it up to someone who needs it more.

Not being able to say no stems from mental misconceptions, from thoughts that your mind has led you to believe are true.

Awareness to Embrace: Saying no is a benefit to others.

Often, guilt arises about saying no because you think about the challenges you could cause for others, when in fact, there are benefits to both you *and* to the other person. We don't say no because we only see one side of the picture. So, to get over the discomfort when you want to make a different choice, here is what you do.

Make four columns on a piece of paper. In the first column, write down the benefits to you if you say no. In column two, write the disadvantages to you if you say yes. In column three, write the disadvantages to the other person if you say yes. In column four, write the advantages to the other person if you say no. The first two columns are easy, but the last two are where the magic happens. As you start to see the bigger picture arise, the full reality, you can begin to find a new way to take action.

Mission to Power:

1. Be honest with yourself.

Start to acknowledge to yourself what you really want to do. Don't make excuses like, "Well, it won't take that long." Or "I should because I have more time." Or "I can't leave them in the lurch like that." The key is to be completely honest with yourself about how you feel. No buts. No thoughts like, "You shouldn't feel this way." Own your feelings.

2. Give yourself permission.

It's never easy to make changes. You need to set things up so that you have the best chance of success, so it's important to give yourself permission to make this change. If you've been taught that you should always help family or that you must always accommodate, while this may be true in some situations, it's not true for you in all situations. Give yourself permission to say no when something doesn't work for you. It's much better to say yes to a request for help because of a choice rather than because you felt bad saying no.

3. Be ready to say no.

Have some phrases ready to buy you time. Practice them so that when you need to pull them out, they are there, ready to say. If the person asking is someone who knows you well, say something like, "Last week I made a commitment to start some things I've been putting off forever. I'm really sorry, but for the next couple of weeks I won't be available." When a few weeks have passed, then you can maintain that you don't have the time.

Some other ideas: "That sounds great, but I'm going to have to say no." Follow up by saying you are taking some time off from social activities, and then, "Let me think about it (or check my schedule) and get back to you." Or, "Thank you for asking, but I'm not able to commit to that. I'll let you know if I can think of anyone." The main thing is for you to have something prepared in your head.

4. Make it a habit to consider all sides of any request.

Remember that your time and your energy belong to you. Anytime you are faced with a request and want to say no but are having a hard time, write out the list of benefits to you and advantages to the other person of saying no. This helps you to get out of the mindset of feeling bad because you think you *should*. With these tools and your desire to make a change, you will be more empowered to speak your truth.

Affirmations for Strength:

- My time and energy are mine to give or to keep, as I choose.
- The more I focus on myself, the more inspired I become about life.
- I will not veer from my heart-inspired desires, even if I have many hurdles along the way.

INDECISIVENESS

Associated Archetypes: If you have or Wood (Nexus), Earth (Talitha), or Metal (Alcor) as a primary or secondary archetype, you may relate to having an issue with indecisiveness when you are stressed.

What: Indecisiveness can be chronic, or it may occur only when you are faced with making a big life decision, but no matter when it happens, it is uncomfortable and makes you feel stuck. As well, what causes indecisiveness in you might not be the same as what triggers someone else, however, a few key things are usually at the core. You may be trying to please someone, have fears about making a mistake, or you may not trust your own judgment.

Awareness to Embrace: There are strategies that can help immensely when you are faced with a decision.

Even if you have labeled yourself as indecisive or have long-standing issues around making decisions, decisiveness is a skill that you can learn. When practiced over time, you can get better at it in the same way that you got better as you practiced typing, driving, or operating an unfamiliar computer program. Decisiveness is a skill.

Mission to Power:

1. Name the fear or fears that are causing you to be indecisive.

When faced with a major decision, we are often indecisive because we are afraid. If this is you, ask yourself what the worst thing is that could happen? Once you identify the fear, determine what you would do in that situation. Who would you turn to for support? What plans would need to change? What would you gain should your fear come to pass? Where would you find relief? When you get to the core of the fear and define some concrete ways to deal with it, it loses power over you.

2. Stop yourself from overthinking.

Sometimes you just need to let go and remind yourself that no matter what decision you make, you will be fine. You will get exactly what you need to get, and there is no "wrong" decision. Contrary to what we think, it's almost impossible to calculate future outcomes accurately because people and life are unpredictable. We really don't have control over all outcomes, so choose what seems the best option given what you know today, and then trust that things will unfold perfectly.

3. What does your heart say?

It is possible to get stuck between the chatter of the mind and what you really feel is the right decision. Sometimes we know what we want but are just afraid of a bad outcome and start doubting. When push comes to shove, following your heart will usher you onto a new playing field. It's also wise to remember that within your heart is a wealth of knowledge integrated with validated facts that you can access at a critical crossroad.

4. Erase the *should* part of it.

Often, we worry about what others might think, which makes us to want to satisfy both the people important to us and ourselves. This influence is confusing and can keep you going back and forth between two choices. At the very least, take out the *should* part and ask yourself what *you* would choose. Be clear about this; it can help you when you need to make the decision. At least you'll know what the underlying influence is.

5. When all else fails, flip a coin—literally.

When you are at an impasse and your top two choices seem to have equal pros and cons, then let the Universe decide, literally. Use a coin to break your mental logjam. When you can't decide, it's either because you can't choose between two negative options or two equal courses of action. Flipping a coin can at least get you to commit to a path of action.

Affirmations for Strength:

- I make choices that are right for me. The more I value myself, the more valuable I am to others.
- My life is coming together in perfect alignment. Any fears I have are an imperfect view of an incomplete reality.
- I expand my thinking beyond what I believe is possible. I take my focus off the obstacles and look towards my vision.

INSECURITY

Associated Archetypes: If you have Water (Selene) or Earth (Talitha) as a primary or secondary archetype, you may relate to the weakness of insecurity.

What: Insecurity is simply a lack of confidence in yourself and a lack of trust in who you are and how you contribute value. When you are insecure about something, you judge yourself negatively in that area and rely on others to affirm your value. No matter where your insecurity shows up, whether in relationships, in specific situations, or around certain groups of people, it's because you are making irrational interpretations about yourself or about your ability to do something. Anytime you believe you are "not good enough," you will worry about being judged, rejected, or criticized. Your insecurity may show up in several forms: arrogance, selfishness, combativeness, defensiveness, or judgmentalism.

Awareness to Embrace: You are insecure because your internal fears have created a flawed reality.

Your insecurity stems from irrational interpretations you have made about you or your abilities. Likely, many of these are based on your past. If you were criticized a lot growing up, it's natural to be critical of yourself and to compare yourself unfavorably to others. For example, if you were often told you were dumb—even if you are the smartest person in the room and even if you have evidence showing that you are—you will still feel insecure relative to others whom you see as smart.

If you need approval to feel secure, then it's likely that you were not given the acknowledgement you needed in the past. When people abandon us, we learn not to trust, and this can be the origin of our insecurity as we grow. The key is to realize that whatever you are insecure about is simply a flawed reality that you can change by changing your focus.

Mission to Power:

1. Visit the past for clues.

Uncover the irrational beliefs and unhelpful thinking that are at the core of your insecurities. Were your insecurities shaped by a parent or other authority figure? Often the outer voices we heard growing up seamlessly become the inner critical voices that speak to us long after we are away from those people. Whether you were criticized or over-praised, the imbalance is what leads to insecurity.

Answer these questions:

- What do I feel insecure about?
- What does the critical inner voice say?
- When do I hear it?
- Who or what am I comparing myself to?

What group of memories have you held onto that currently influence your feelings about yourself? How you interpret these experiences is what makes you feel the way you do. At the heart of it all is a set of limiting beliefs or unhelpful thoughts that you have chosen to adopt. Now is the time to un-adopt them.

2. Use your powers of objectivity and reasoning.

Insecurities are based on your interpretation of situations, circumstances, or people in your life. They are simply opinions and perspectives that you have decided are true. Take a moment to challenge your insecurities. It's the only way you can change your perspective.

Ask yourself:

- Is what I see true, or is it just what I imagine to be true?
- How else could I interpret this situation?
- How else could I view myself and where I stand in this situation?
- How would someone else see me and describe this?

The only way to open the door to new perspectives is by challenging yourself to think objectively and question the validity of your experiences.

3. Stop judging yourself so harshly.

We judge others, but we also judge ourselves. One way to move towards greater self-acceptance (and less insecurity) is to actively practice being non-judgmental. When you find that you are forming a judgment about yourself or others, stop and ask who you are comparing yourself (or them) to, and why you would think that. Follow it up by finding something to compliment about the person or situation.

For example, let's say you think, "I'm not as experienced as the other people here. I'm so out of my league. People are going to wonder why I'm even here." Noticing that, tell yourself something like this to counter it: "Well, I did have the courage to show up. I'll likely learn something, and I look forward to offering a different perspective to the group." Then, think of a situation in which you are an expert. How would you feel if there was someone in the group who was not as experienced as you? Would it be as big a deal as you feel it is?

Affirmations for Strength:

- I choose to expand my thinking about myself beyond my perceived reality.

- I focus on my attributes and the way I contribute to every person and situation.

- I accept myself as I am. Any insecurity I feel is from an imperfect view of an incomplete reality.

LOW SELF-ESTEEM

Associated Archetypes: If you have Water (Selene) or Earth (Talitha) as a primary or secondary archetype, you may relate to having the weakness of low self-esteem.

What: Simply put, low self-esteem is the result of not appreciating and accepting yourself for who you are. As a result, virtually every facet of your life, including your relationships, your job, and even your health, is negatively affected. When you have healthy self-esteem, you accept and appreciate yourself for who you are, even as you acknowledge your perceived faults, weaknesses, and inabilities. The difference between those with good self-esteem and those with low self-esteem has nothing to do with measurable ability. Healthy self-esteem is a matter of embracing and acknowledging both your strengths *and* your weaknesses and moving through the world safe in that knowledge.

Awareness to Embrace: We are all born with infinite potential and equal worth. If you think anything less than that of yourself, it's something you've learned over time.

It is possible to raise your self-esteem—even if you've had a poor opinion of yourself since you were a child. Through mindfulness, being kinder to yourself, and redirecting your self-destructive thoughts, you can unlearn some of the beliefs about yourself that you've adopted over time. It doesn't matter whether you believe that your value comes from the physical (how you look or what you own) or from accomplishments, you can raise it.

The most important thing to realize about self-worth is that there is only one opinion that matters—yours. We are our own harshest critics, so the first step towards change is to evaluate how you see yourself.

Mission to Power:

1. Take a self-esteem inventory.

You can't change what you don't know when it comes to self-esteem. Start by defining ten strengths and ten weaknesses that you see in yourself. If you have difficulty thinking of strengths, ponder what others have said to you over the years: "Thanks for listening to me the other night" (you're a good listener) or "You really helped us with that project. Thanks for pitching in" (you're willing to help out).

Even if you think a strength is insignificant, list it anyway. Write down where you see you have value or provide value: your skills, experiences, physical and social resources, talents, and anything else that makes you feel good about yourself.

It's usually easier to come up with weaknesses, since we notice our weaknesses when we compare ourselves to others. These are things the inner critic says about you not being good enough. They could be about your physical appearance, your inability to do something well, or areas in which you feel inadequate.

Your self-esteem inventory lets you know all the things you already tell yourself about how good or "bad" you are.

2. Set your intent to be mindful and to refocus.

By nature, we humans tend to focus on the negative, and the more we focus on the negative, the more it becomes the reality by which we define ourselves. When you catch yourself focusing on some perceived "lack," you can build confidence and esteem by noting where you have the opposite. For example, if you notice you are focusing on not being a good conversationalist while at a big party, you might remind yourself that you are very good with people one on one. Everyone is confident in some area of life, yet we often minimize it because we are comparing ourselves to other people and have unrealistic expectations. So again, when you notice that you are thinking about not being "good enough," stop and confirm an area in which you have confidence in yourself.

You are a "package," and not just one item. Therefore, when a shortcoming gets highlighted in your mind, remind yourself that you are a multi-faceted package. And then, take a moment to remind yourself of all the problems you have faced and tackled. Building your self-esteem takes time, and only you can do it; you do it by changing your focus and what you notice about yourself.

3. Stop comparing yourself to others (Law of Relativity).

Nothing can hurt your self-esteem more than unfair comparisons. "John is smarter in business." "Mary has a bigger house than I do." "Susie is prettier than me." "Joe is younger and makes more money than me." You can see how the more you do this, the more it is bound to affect your feelings about yourself.

The solution: you must *decide* to stop comparing yourself to others. The only person to compare yourself to is you. Notice how far you've come, areas in which you've grown, or how you have improved. What is more, these comparisons are unfair because you don't know what it is really like to be that other person. You think it's better, but it may be a hundred times worse than you can imagine.

Answer these questions as abundantly as you can for a powerful shift in perspective:

- Who praises you and shows you love, befriends you, and cares about you, even though you don't look the way you want to?
- Who do you love even though they don't look like their most awesome selves?
- Who do you admire and respect even though they don't fit the classic mold of "beautiful?"
- Who is beautiful physically (with looks "to die for") but is someone you would no way in hell trade places with because of things you see in their personality that turn you off?

Affirmations for Strength:

- I see value in all I do and all I am.
- I set up realistic expectations of myself and choose to compare myself to myself.
- I decide who I am. I give myself permission to be the master of my own life and my own reality.

NEGATIVE THINKING

Associated Archetypes: All archetypes need to be attentive to excessive negative thinking, but if you have Fire (Avior), Wood (Nexus), or Metal (Alcor) as a primary or secondary archetype, when imbalanced, you may relate to negative thinking as a weakness.

What: Negative thinking is a tendency to believe the worst in any situation or to lower your expectations by considering worst possible scenarios. Negative thinking is a protective mechanism; it can be useful when you are balanced, which means when you are also considering positive outcomes or options. Consistently focusing on the negative can become a habit that distorts reality and causes unnecessary stress, worry, sadness, or even depression.

Awareness to Embrace: Negative thinking is a habit, and you can change habits.

You can let go of the habit of negative thinking by, first, noticing your negative thoughts, and second, practicing positive thinking. The mistake people often make is to think that they must stop their negative thoughts. Thought-stopping doesn't work; the more you try to stop your negative thoughts from occurring, the more negative thoughts you'll have. For example, if I tell you not to think of a green cat, you will not be able to stop thinking of a green cat. Trying not to think a thought causes the thought to persist.

The strategy is to allow your negative thoughts to surface, acknowledge them, and then choose new ways to see the situations that are eliciting your negative thoughts.

Mission to Power:

1. Recognize when your thoughts are distorted and inaccurate.

Inaccurate thoughts reinforce negative thinking. If you can recognize them, you can challenge them. Our minds have ways to convince us of things that are not true. Do you have any of the following thought distortions?

Filtering: Do you focus on only one negative aspect of a situation and ignore everything else that's positive? If you catch yourself doing this, force yourself to look at the good side. For example, if someone says you missed something minor on a project, don't keep thinking that the whole project is ruined. Instead of focusing on the mistake, note everything else that you did well.

Personalizing: Do you automatically take blame for things? If someone doesn't return your greeting as warmly as usual, do you think you must have done something to upset them? Instead, look for other reasons. Maybe the person just received some bad news that has nothing to do with you.

Jumping to Conclusions: Do you imagine the worst possible option? For example, let's say you didn't get a call back right away so you decide that the person must not want you for the position you applied for. After noticing this thought, find other reasons for not getting an immediate callback. Perhaps the person was busy. Perhaps the person who makes the decision had an emergency. Look for possible conclusions that are positive.

Mind Reading: Do you assume that you know what others are thinking and fail to consider other likely possibilities? For example, you go to an event and think, "People are wondering what I'm doing here," when, in fact, it's likely that no one cares.

2. Notice whether you are more negative than you think.

Here are some examples of how you might be speaking and thinking negatively without realizing it.

Negative: "A job that pays more would be great, but I'd probably have to drive further, deal with expensive parking, and end up working with people I don't like."

Better: "A job that pays more would be great. Some things will have to change, but I'm sure I'll adapt well."

Negative: "My husband took out the trash tonight, finally, after nagging him forever. How hard is it to do something so simple?"

Better: "My husband took out the trash tonight, finally. The kitchen looks so much better without the bags of trash."

Negative: "Ugh. I hate all the morning traffic. It takes forever to get to work and all I deal with are stupid drivers."

Better: "Ugh. I hate all the morning traffic. Then again, it does give me a chance to think about the day, make calls if I need to, and listen to some good music."

3. Get the negativity out from around you.

Do you hang around with people who are negative? Do you constantly read the most negative, fear-provoking news? Do your friends complain a lot? Do you get hooked on shows that draw you into the negative? Our culture thrives on negativity, and it's almost impossible to turn on the TV, scroll through social media, or listen to the radio without experiencing some form of negativity.

Be mindful of what you surround yourself with. Think of ways to limit what you take in externally so that you don't perpetuate the negative triggers internally.

4. Practice gratitude. It really does help.

Research shows that being grateful has a huge impact on your outlook, your levels of positivity, as well as your happiness. Even if you are having a very difficult time in life, if you look for what is good, what's supportive, what's going well, and the small, vital things that you *do* have, then your brain will rewire itself to see what's good, leading to a sense of balance or calm. At the end of the day, find three specific things that went well. Affirming them has been proven to shift a negative reality to a more positive one. If we see good, we feel good.

Affirmations for Strength:

- I naturally focus on what's good, what's working, and where I am loved and supported in my life.

- I surround myself with people who affect my life positively and gently release those who drain my energy.

- My perspective is completely in my control. My power lies in seeing my challenges as benefits.

OVERWHELM

Associated Archetypes: If you have Water (Selene), Earth (Talitha), or Metal (Alcor) as a primary or secondary archetype, you may have a tendency to easily become overwhelmed.

What: Overwhelm arises when you feel you have too much to deal with—so much so that it feels paralyzing. For so much of human history, our lives were shaped by shortages—food, water, shelter, tools, clothing. Everything we needed had to be sourced, made, or found. Because of this, our brains are comfortable with lack and scarcity. These days, with everything in "more" mode, we feel we need to do more, be more, handle more, and get more done. The result is overwhelm on an extraordinary scale.

Awareness to Embrace: We do not get overwhelmed because what of what we are doing, but because of what we are feeling.

It is possible to have many things on your plate and still feel calm, centered, and poised. What makes our lives seem overwhelming depends a lot on our perceptions, habits, and the labels we put on things. The feeling you experience when you are overwhelmed is simply a state of mind that you have created. The good thing is that you *do* have control over your state of mind.

At the end of the day, make it a point to consciously recognize what you have accomplished instead of noticing all the things you still have to do.

Mission to Power:

1. Stop "hating" time.

Time is not your enemy. How many times in a day do you think, "There's not enough time" or "I just don't have the time." It would be wise to change your mind-set about time, because optimal productivity cannot emerge from a place of busyness coupled with thoughts of overwhelm. Can you remember times where you were extremely productive in a very short time? We all get a lot done when we have a limited amount of time in which to do it. The important thing for you to realize is that feeling overwhelmed is not about time. Begin to change your mind-set about time, and you'll create more space as you grow in this awareness.

2. Regularly affirm your productivity.

How you think of what's going on in your life makes a big difference. When we are overwhelmed, we only think about what we didn't do, where we are behind, what we still need to finish, and so on, and rarely do we think about how we have been productive. *Productive* is the key word. The feeling of productivity has been tested, and it is one of the best feelings in the world. So, whether you are a manager, a busy mother, a business owner, or someone who is self-governing, affirm the ways in which you have been productive. How you think about what you have done makes a big difference in your perception of overwhelm.

3. Manage your shoulds.

Overwhelm also comes from within your mind in the form of too many *shoulds*. Are you telling yourself that you *should* do this or that? Do you say things like, "I should keep my house cleaner," "I should eat healthier," or "I should call my mother more often?" Even though you think these things and likely believe them to be important, you won't do them because your perception of the gain isn't strong enough.

Let's say you glance at a drawer and think, "I should clean out that messy drawer." Once you think it, the task exists in two places—physically and in your mind—and every time you see that drawer, you are negatively reminded that you *should* do it. Your *shoulds* create mental clutter that adds to overwhelm.

Next time you hear yourself remarking that you *should* do something, catch yourself and refocus. Stop and affirm that you will do it when the time is right, and that you do the things that are truly priority.

4. Get it out of your head.

Sometimes the best thing you can do is take thirty minutes to do a "brain dump." This is where you sit down with a blank piece of paper and write down every single thing that you must do, committed to do, or forgot you needed to do; the people you need to see, calls you need to make, places you have to go, things you need to fix, projects you need to research, and so on.

Write it all in one column, big things and small things, and use as many pieces of paper as you need. When you think you're finished, don't stop. Wait a few minutes, take a few deep breaths, and you'll be surprised to find that more will come. Do this for every area of your life. You can organize it later, so for now just write what comes out in any order that the thoughts come.

Next, read through the list. Note that some of the items are *shoulds* and do not need your attention right now, while others are priority.

Mark five priority *must dos* for today or this week with a star, and decide when you are going to do them. Once you put the task in your schedule, you'll feel better.

Next, if there are things that can wait to be addressed in a future week or month, write the month next to them and remove them from their place in your current overwhelm. Put them in your calendar. If there is anything to delegate, write a *D* next to it and schedule time to delegate.

If there are any *shoulds,* put an *X* by them. Since they didn't fall into your priorities for a future week or month, you'll get to them when you need to.

You might see some tasks that don't need to be done, at all. You have been carrying them around in your head, and now you can get rid of them. Cross them out!

By this time, you will likely be feeling much lighter—more space in your head, more air in your lungs, and more energy to start moving forward again.

Affirmations for Strength:

- I stay present in each moment and focus on the task at hand.
- I am becoming wiser each day and I trust in my ability to master my life.
- I set up realistic expectations of myself and others so that I may thrive.

PEOPLE PLEASING

Associated Archetypes: If you have Water (Selene) or Earth (Talitha) as a primary or secondary archetype, you may relate to the weakness of being a people pleaser.

What: People pleasing stems from wanting everyone around you to be happy and doing whatever it takes to keep the peace. It might be that you say yes as a habit; it might be that you have a need to be needed; maybe you say yes because you don't want to disappoint or let down another's expectations of you. People pleasers need others to validate them; their security depends on getting approval. Basically, people pleasing is caused by a lack of confidence.

Awareness to Embrace: Putting yourself first is not selfish, although you may believe it is consciously or subconsciously.

As a people pleaser, you may feel that you are being selfish when you honor your own needs. This mind-set is the best place to start working on change. When you take care of yourself first, you can care for others from a place of inner abundance. When you feel taken care of from within, you have more to give.

Many people pleasers associate being "good" with putting themselves second. This kind of thinking not only lessens your self-value in the eyes of others, but it also makes it very easy for you to build up resentment. Taking care of your needs is not an option, it's a necessity. When others ask things of you, or you feel you "have to" devote personal time or energy to avoid conflict, remind yourself that when you overextend, no one wins, least of all you. Finally, remind yourself that the energy you are giving is *your* energy.

Mission to Power:

1. Before you say yes, remember that you have a choice.

You may feel you don't have a choice, that you have to say yes, but really, you do have a choice. When you people please, you are choosing to avoid conflict, or to seem accommodating, or so that you can be the "hero" who saves the day. You're doing it for a reason, so, if you want to change that reason, you will first have to recognize that you *do* have a choice.

2. Stall whenever you are asked to do something.

Since people pleasers generally agree out of habit, buy yourself some time when you are asked for something. "I'll think about it," or, "I'll get back to you on that as soon as I can" are phrases that give you the time and space to consider what you are being asked to do. Will it be stressful? Do you actually have the time to do it? If you say yes, are you likely to be upset with the person who asked?

Stalling is an invaluable tactic, because otherwise, once you say yes, you're not only stuck, you start wondering what you were thinking.

3. Consider whether the person is manipulating you.

Is this person taking advantage of you? People often use compliments or other means to coax you to do something: "You're so organized—you're the perfect person to handle this." Or, "You're the only one who can do this!" Or, "You said you're really into this kind of thing, and your husband said you're free that day." (If you think this is true, ask yourself whether you really want to agree.)

4. Remember, saying no is never as bad as you think it will be.

Most people pleasers worry that when they say no, the result is going to be really bad, but that's more a figment of your imagination as you dwell on the worst, because it's never as bad as you think. If you say no, and if you mean it, the asker will move on, looking for someone else. You might feel bad or guilty for saying no, but remember, the upside is that you are claiming and valuing your time.

5. Do not give excuses or reasons for saying no.

When you say no, there is no reason to defend your decision so that the other understands why you refused. It's tempting to justify why you have no time or can't do something well, but that only opens up the door for the person to counter your refusal with something like: "Oh, that's okay. You can do it later when you have time." Or, "It doesn't have to be perfect; I just need it done."

Affirmations for Strength:

- I allow the enlightened part of me to be my guide rather than the part of me that fears a negative outcome.
- I spend my time, money, resources, and energy wisely. I am productive in the areas I want to be, and I bring the best of who I am to the table of life.
- I make choices that are right for me. The more I value myself, the greater my value to others.

PROCRASTINATION

Associated Archetypes: If you have Water (Selene), Earth (Talitha), or Metal (Alcor) as a primary or secondary archetype, you may relate to the issue of procrastination.

What: Procrastination is the act of delaying or postponing something that you know you must do eventually. Human beings have been procrastinating for hundreds of years. It's such a part of who we are that Greek philosophers as far back as Plato developed the word *akrasia* to describe this behavior. Akrasia is a state in which you do things against your better judgment—like surfing the Internet instead of working on your project or watching TV instead of doing the laundry. Loosely translated, *akrasia* is lack of self-control. It's the force that takes you away from what you intended to do.

Awareness to Embrace: Procrastination happens when you are not inspired by the task you know you *must* do.

When you really want to do something, you find the time, money, and energy to do it. You don't procrastinate because, intrinsically, you know you will get more *gain* from it than the *pain* it takes to get going. We procrastinate when we are not inspired to do something that we know we *have to* do.

We've all suffered from bouts of procrastination, and probably the worst part is its uncanny ability to rob us of our time while simultaneously making us feel guilty about it. Even though we dread what we are avoiding, not doing it doesn't provide any relief, since deep down we know we are just delaying the inevitable.

Interestingly, research suggests that one of the most effective ways to overcome procrastination is to forgive yourself for procrastinating. Since procrastination is linked to negative feelings, forgiveness can reduce the guilt you feel about procrastinating, which is one of the main triggers for procrastinating in the first place.

Mission to Power:

1. Don't wait until you "feel like it."

Pick up a project that you've been putting off and commit to doing it for just ten minutes. Don't wait for your mood to match the task (because it never will). Start the task and, once there is momentum, progress becomes satisfying and addictive and you're more likely to finish.

Although delaying can temporarily boost your mood, over time, it actually works against you. When you give in to feeling good in the moment instead of what's in your own best interest, you make it more likely that you will keep putting things off. Aphorist Mason Cooley said, "Procrastination makes easy things hard, and hard things harder." (Just think about the dishes you leave overnight and have to face in the morning.)

2. Get started by setting new success goals.

We are not machines. As creatures that crave instant gratification, a series of short-term goals and rewards makes it easier to start. Why? Because the friction around starting something that we aren't inspired by is what causes us to procrastinate.

To make it easier to start anything that you've been putting off, give yourself permission to work on it for only three minutes. Instead of saying, "I have to start exercising," just decide to put on your workout clothes. Instead of thinking, "I have to read this book," decide to read only one page. Instead of fretting, "I have to get that report done!" collect all the information you need to begin. Instead of just saying, "I have to meditate more," decide to meditate for three minutes right then.

This is a great way to move from procrastination into action. Once you start on the path of what you've been resisting, it's much easier to see it to completion. Starting this way will not only make you feel better; it will also increase the likelihood that the task will get done.

3. Prioritize by making a list.

To spend time on what is truly important first, you must define your priorities. If you keep spending time on things that are small but urgent, life becomes about putting out fires rather than expanding horizons. Small measures of progress coupled with direction will help you to maintain momentum over time.

Having a system is key. At the end of the day, write down five things that you need to accomplish the next day. If you don't get a chance to do this at night, then do it first thing in the morning. Do not write down more than five to dos." Now, prioritize them in order of importance. When it's time to get to work, start from the top priority and work down. At the end of the day, move any unfinished tasks to a new list.

Studies have shown that the speed at which you complete your first task holds special importance for overcoming procrastination and maintaining high productivity throughout the day.

Affirmations for Strength:

- I am a master of the moment, and I make decisions that allow me to thrive.

- My goal is to be present in every moment and to realize that my current actions determine my future happiness.

- I set realistic expectations of myself and others to avoid disappointment.

RESENTMENT

Associated Archetypes: If you have Wood (Nexus), Fire (Avior), or Metal (Alcor) as a primary or secondary archetype, you may have a tendency to hold resentment.

What: Resentment is both a state of mind and a bodily feeling. It's a form of anger that results from a real or imagined injustice or an unfulfilled, possibly unrealistic, expectation. You hold onto resentment when you associate more negatives than positives with an expected outcome or behavior. Often, it's because you build your expectations on the foundation of a distorted belief that others will act the way you want them to.

Without knowing it, you may still be carrying around negative feelings or resentment over something in the past, even if you think you're "over it." The original anger might have been forgotten, but the repressed resentment is still there, unbalanced and unresolved. Past unresolved resentments can influence and impair the way you interact with others in the present. This is a form of mental and emotional bondage.

Awareness to Embrace: Your resentments are not personal, they are instructional. Everything in life is a lesson, and it's your perception that keeps the grudge alive.

You can't let go of resentment until you change your perception of the situation that led to it in the first place. Resentments will not dissipate as long as you consciously or subconsciously judge a situation as more bad than good. However, there is a way to face resentments and heal from them, even if the resentment you are holding onto is deep-seated and from long ago.

By balancing out the emotional charge you have concerning a situation, you can free yourself from the stress and the resentment you've been carrying around both consciously and subconsciously.

Mission to Power:

1. Make a list of every person towards whom you have resentment.

This list is to include anyone past or present toward whom you have a negative feeling because of an unmet expectation. The list can include very small things, such as someone not thanking you for something you went out of your way to do, or it might be toward someone you supported and later discovered didn't do what you thought they should have.

2. Next to each person's name, identify what they did.

This part requires you to sit with the uncomfortable emotions that arise when you visit old memories or think about unpleasant current situations.

Next to the person's name, write exactly what the person did that caused you to feel the way you do about them. Is it because you weren't appreciated? Because they always took the attention away from you? Because they made you feel inadequate? Because they seemingly have a better life? Because they never repaid you or they spoke poorly of you? It doesn't have to make sense, it just has to be your truth.

3. Contemplate how each action affects you.

If you resent someone for taking attention away from you, it affected your self-esteem. If it's because they took you for granted, it affected your self-value. If it's because they never asked your opinion or advice, it affected your self-worth and made you feel that you had nothing to contribute.

The point of this exercise is to make you specifically aware of how these people have affected your self-identity and your ability to feel safe, confident, and secure about who you are.

4. How did you benefit? What is your gain?

You know the negative part, but until you can see the equilibrating, positive side, your focus will remain on the downside of the person, and your limited perception keeps the grudge alive.

Let's start with the idea that every action has two sides—a benefit and a drawback. If you begin listing the positives you've received because of a situation with someone, your initial anger will soften and dissipate, because you'll see that you were not just a victim, but that you also personally gained in a way that you did not initially see.

For example, because a person didn't appreciate you, did you start drawing stronger boundaries around your time? Or, if a friend didn't pay you back, did you develop new rules about letting friends borrow money? Did any of the situations cause you to rethink not speaking up for yourself? In fact, we gain and grow from every situation in our lives.

5. When have you done the same thing to someone else?

Your first thought may be that you have never done this to anyone or that you wouldn't ever do something like this, but take a deep breath and open your heart to the possibilities. Where might you have done this same thing to someone else without even realizing it? Do you sometimes take attention away from others? Have you ever failed to ask someone's opinion or advice even though you didn't have anything against them? Have you ever taken someone for granted? The key is to see that what you dislike and are holding against someone is something you too have done.

Affirmations for Strength:

- I am a master at seeing and accepting the two sides of every situation, and I embrace both as life helps me grow.

- How I see all situations in my life is in my mind and in my control.

- I give myself permission to be the master of my life.

SELF-DOUBT

Associated Archetypes: If you have Water (Selene), Wood (Nexus), or Earth (Talitha) as a primary or secondary archetype, you may tend to doubt yourself.

What: Self-doubt is the troubling, yet persuasive inner voice that holds you back from making progress and seizing opportunities by pointing out all the ways you can't do what you set out to do. It makes doing things much harder than they need to be. Unless you curb your self-doubt, your destructive thoughts will drive you to surrender and believe them true. You see, doubts don't leave you alone. What starts out as the voice of reason from parents and other authorities becomes, over time, the doubtful inner critic.

By the time we reach adulthood, studies show that we will have heard the word *no* 50,000 times and the word *yes* an average of 7,000 times. It's no wonder that negativity and self-doubt creep into our minds.

Awareness to Embrace: Self-doubt is actively maintained through the way you think.

The good news is that you can lower self-doubt and increase your confidence by shifting your focus. We maintain self-doubt in three ways: selective attention, selective memory, and selective interpretation.

Selective attention means that you tend to notice situations that confirm your lack of value or downplay your strengths. If someone says, "Wow, you did that so well!" you say, "It was no big deal." Or they say, "Thanks for your help" and you say, "It was nothing," even though you put in a lot of time and effort.

Selective memory is failing to remember the times you were successful or did something worthwhile.

Selective interpretation is interpreting things in a way that affirms your low value. For example, if someone doesn't call you back, you assume that you're not important to them or that they're upset with you. You make sense of things based on your insecurity rather than the reality.

Mission to Power:

1. Start listening to positive feedback from others.

At first, as per habit, you'll tend to minimize what is said and the importance of it. That's normal, but once you do start noticing the positive feedback, affirm that it exists. How did someone show that you have value? Did they text to say hi? Did someone bring you a snack? Affirm positive things for yourself, as well. Did you complete something, help someone, or were you friendly to someone? Take note of everything.

2. Begin creating different interpretations of events.

When someone does something and you notice that you are looking at it from an insecure point of view, ask yourself if there is another way to make sense of the situation. How else can you look at it? If someone doesn't return your call right away, is it because they haven't had a chance to do so? Perhaps it's an especially busy time. What are other possible reasons that don't have to do with you? If your partner, co-worker, or boss is quieter than usual in your presence, instead of thinking that you did something wrong, ask yourself if it is possible the withdrawal *might be* due to something that had nothing to do with you.

3. Remember that people don't really care that much about what you do.

If you are the type who worries about what others may think about you, then self-doubt can creep in and take hold, rendering you incapable of moving forward with confidence. Whenever you start doubting yourself because of what others may think about you, remind yourself that most people care more about themselves, their kids, their projects, and their lives.

4. Remind yourself of the Law of Relativity

The universal Law of Relativity states that nothing is good or bad or big or small until we compare it to something else. Everything we are and everything in our lives just *is*—until we start comparing. In other words, nothing in life has any meaning except for the meaning we give it.

This universal law is about accepting yourself as an individual within the collective and recognizing that comparing yourself to others does not serve you—because there is nothing to compare. Many of us were conditioned in childhood to think that we should be the same as others; because of this, we compare and judge our beauty, success, happiness, finances, and love against what everyone else has, and this allows self-doubt to take hold. Better is to compare yourself to yourself. Note how far you've come and where you've made progress.

Affirmations for Strength:

- I see my own value everywhere I look, which increases my confidence.

- I focus on my strengths, my accomplishments, and my areas of success.

- I decide where I want to play in the game of life. I give myself permission to be the master of my life.

STRESS

Associated Archetypes: Although, of course, all people experience stress, if you have Wood (Nexus), Fire (Avior), or Metal (Alcor) as a primary or secondary archetype, you may relate to having an issue with stress.

What: Stress is the inability to adapt to a changing environment. The less adaptable you are to change, the more stress you experience. Basically, stress is your body's way of responding to a situation or a demand that exceeds what you feel is your ability to cope. Stress is part of being human; we all feel it from time to time. Stress can be beneficial when it produces the incentive you need to get you through deadline situations, yet too much stress is not only uncomfortable and undesirable, it negatively impacts your body. Studies have shown that 70 - 90 percent of doctor visits are linked to stress.

Awareness to Embrace: It's not what happens to you, it's how you perceive what may or may not happen that counts.

It's common to perceive only the negative side of an event that's stressing you, further promoting the stress you are experiencing and keeping you perpetually bound to the so-called stressor. We are told that stress is bad for us, but did you know that there are positive aspects to stress, as well?

A study was done in which half the participants in a group were informed about the benefits of stress, and the other half were informed about the dangers of stress. The group that was told the positive aspects changed how they perceived stress, and their symptoms of stress decreased by 23 percent in a short time. This study shows that our perceptions about stress can make a big difference. So, then, what are the beneficial aspects of stress?

Hormones released by stress response boost performance on memory, facilitate mental toughness, deepen social bonds, strengthen priorities, and increase the speed at which the brain processes information.

Mission to Power:

1. Balance your perception of what's stressing you by discovering how it's serving you.

Since it's not what happens to you but how you perceive what may or may not happen that creates stress, take some time to think about how your stress is benefiting you. The more positives you can assign to your stressful situation, the more balanced you will feel. When you can see that what's going on can work to your advantage, your stress dissipates.

Our perceptions are what make heaven or hell out of our lives. As such, it's wise to look for what's happening on the other side of your stress. How might this stressor be beneficial to you now or in the future? How is your stressful situation serving you? For example, is the stressful situation helping you stay on track, be productive, build or improve a skill, communicate better with your spouse, bond with your co-workers, etc.? The key to balancing your stress is to balance your perceptions by bringing conscious awareness to the positives.

2. Understand why you get stressed.

The main reason we stress about things is because we care. Explore what you care about and understand your stress in this light, and you will link it to something positive and meaningful. For example, do you care about your reputation? Your example as a role model to your children? Your ability to show competency at work? Not letting the team down? Ensuring that guests enjoy the party you are hosting?

Your stress is always tied to something you care about. Human beings care. You care. You stress because you care. If you didn't care, you wouldn't stress. Caring is a wonderful trait of being human.

3. Stop distorting what you say or think about situations.

Lessen your stress by reducing the following bad habits:

- Stop "all-or-nothing" thinking: Looking at things from a black-or-white perspective and not allowing yourself to see a balanced reality increases stress. For example, thinking, "If this doesn't go perfectly, it's going to be all my fault," instead of, "I'll do the best I can."

- Watch out for overgeneralization: When you overgeneralize from a single negative experience and expect it to hold true forever, you set yourself up for stress. For example, "I didn't get hired. I'll never get hired anywhere."

- Be aware of your mental filter: Notice when you are focusing on the negatives and filtering out all the positives. When you notice everything that went wrong but fail to give equal attention to all the things that went right, you set yourself up for a stressful reality.

– Don't diminish the positive: When things go well, don't come up with reasons for why it doesn't count. For example, "The presentation went well, but I was lucky." Own your luck!

– Don't take responsibility for things that are not in your control. For example, "It's my fault he got in an accident. I should have warned him to drive carefully in the rain."

Affirmations for Strength:

• How I see things is in my mind and in my control.

• I set up realistic expectations of myself and others to avoid disappointment.

• There is a bigger picture to all I am going through, and it supports me in every way.

STUBBORNNESS

Associated Archetypes: If you have Fire (Avior), Wood (Nexus), or Metal (Alcor) as a primary or secondary archetype, you may tend to be stubborn.

What: Stubbornness is deep resistance to change. It is a coping strategy used when you have a need for stability and predictability. If you know you are stubborn, or if you've been told that you are, it can manifest positively as being decisive, loyal, and able to stand your ground. But when you are stubborn to the point of closing yourself off from new growth experiences or being unable to collaborate with others, your inflexibility is a disadvantage.

Awareness to Embrace: At the root of stubbornness is fear of change.

Since life is all about change, inflexibility at its core is a resistance to life and its opportunities. If you are over-sensitive to the possibility of change—even change that is for your own good—you will benefit from practicing flexibility. Here are some signs to notice in your behavior when you might be losing out on opportunities:

- You insist on making your point even when you know you are wrong.

- You point out why something won't work when others bring up an idea or make plans.

- You get very angry, frustrated, or impatient when others try to get you to do something or agree with something they are presenting.

- You deny that there is a need for change, and refuse to change when asked to do so.

Mission to Power:

1. Make it a point to listen.

Remind yourself that listening and trying to understand where the other person is coming from does not mean that you have to agree, make immediate changes, or do what they say. Instead of automatically tuning out when someone suggests change, listen and try to understand, so that even if you choose not to, at least you're coming from a place of choice and understanding and not reaction.

2. Remind yourself that there is more than one way.

When you come from a point of stubbornness, you tend to think there is only one way—your way. And because of this, you close down to considering situations openly, possibly losing out on something beneficial for you. Start small. If you can at least look at or allow yourself to explore other alternatives, you move towards greater flexibility. When you open yourself up this way, you might find something better than your original plan.

3. Soften your stance.

When you are "sure" that you are right, it's hard to let go, and being stubborn and saying no upfront can become a habit. In some situations, it may be to your advantage to give a little. Consider how you will gain if you go with a decision or course of action that was not your initial choice. If you usually consider it a "win" to get your way, look at it another way. It could be a "win" to gain the respect of others or to experience the freedom of not having to be responsible for the outcome.

Affirmations for Strength:

- My perspective is completely in my control. My power lies in seeing other options as positive benefits.

- I expand my thinking beyond what I believe is possible. I take my focus off the obstacles to manifest more opportunities.

- I allow the enlightened part of me to be my guide rather than the part of me that fears a negative outcome.

VANITY

Associated Archetypes: If you have Fire (Avior) or Metal (Alcor) as a primary or secondary archetype, you may relate to the weakness of vanity.

What: Vanity shows up in many ways. It is excess concern about others' opinions of us to the detriment of focusing on who we are as a person. Vanity commonly takes the form of being consumed with your appearance or your physical beauty, but it can also take the form of being too concerned with what others think of you or whether they see you as successful. With the prevalence of social media, it is now easy to get caught up in comparisons and thinking that how we look to others is everything.

Awareness to Embrace: One of life's lessons is to accept ourselves as we are.

Accepting yourself means liking yourself and being okay with yourself as you are—without wishing you were taller, skinnier, prettier, smarter, and so on. Truly accepting yourself is one of life's hardest lessons. Our comparisons to others are unrealistic. We have misconceptions about what gives us worth. Note that with your friends—the ones you really love—you don't say that you wish they were skinnier or prettier or richer. You just accept them as they are.

Mission to Power:

1. Start defining yourself in new ways.

Notice the things you value about the people close to you. What is it about them that defines them and makes them special? Do you wish they were prettier? Smarter? Richer? If they were, would you like them more? Likely not. We accept them as they are. Like that, start to look at the things that define you—in addition to your looks or your youth. Focus on the value that you bring to the world through your abilities, personality, and perspective on the world. Be specific and continue to affirm other things about you that are not related to your outer appearance.

2. Take a break from the mirror.

If you have a habit of glancing in the mirror every time you see one to check out how you look, *decide* not to do that and see how it feels. This is a good rule to set for yourself if you often peer at your reflection and give yourself negative feedback. Notice how you feel when you don't give yourself this form of negative feedback.

3. Be realistic.

Who are you comparing yourself to? Are you being fair? Constantly comparing yourself to others who have photo-shopped faces or are younger than you will cause you to feel less than. If you are going to compare yourself, be fair. Compare yourself to a line of people at the supermarket or movie theater, and you'll see that there is no standard of beauty in everyday life.

4. Strive for balance.

We live in a world of balance; inner beauty and outer beauty complement each other. Affirm that anything you do to make yourself attractive on the outside (cosmetic procedures, nice clothing, make-up, hair color, etc.) activates your inner beauty and confidence.

Outer beauty is intrinsically connected to inner beauty. The key is to realize that both types of beauty play a role in activating each other. Mastering both inner beauty and outer beauty is important because, when outer beauty begins to fade, inner beauty will rise.

Affirmations for Strength:

- How I see things is in my mind and in my control.
- The love in my heart and the wisdom I have gained over the years make up the magnificence of who I am.
- I develop my inner beauty and outer beauty and, by doing so, I find deep peace, balance, and stability.

WORRY

Associated Archetypes: Although all of us worry from time to time, if you have Wood (Nexus) or Metal (Alcor) as a primary or secondary archetype, you may relate to having an issue with worry.

What: Worry comes from stories your mind makes up. Worry is rooted in fiction. It's a down payment of energy on a future that may never happen. Worry is one of the most common daily mental activities and the greatest waste of mental energy, not to mention a waste of time.

Subconsciously, you think if you worry enough, what you are worrying about won't happen. Since you are worrying about it in advance, you somehow feel you are protecting yourself from a bad future. Yet, underlying this is the fear that if you let the worry go, the challenge will occur, and then you worry about that. It's a defense mechanism that your brain puts up against the negative events in life, and it is quite complex.

Awareness to Embrace: Worry is a habit that you can break.

Worry is a learned pattern that is handed down, often by parents, and it is completely based on fear and fed by negative thinking. Over time, creating negative scenarios becomes a habit.

To begin the process of breaking the worry habit, the next time you catch yourself worrying about something, consistently affirm the chance that what you are worrying about might not happen at all. The reality is that, at any given moment, something could happen to alter your expected future—anything from winning the lottery to getting a raise to getting fired. The key is to remind yourself of the many possibilities that could unfold, not just the one you are envisioning. A study published in *Clinical Psychology & Psychotherapy* found 85 percent of the things we worry about result in either positive or neutral outcomes. Further, 79 percent of the time when the outcome was negative, the subjects felt they handled the situation better than they had thought they would. This is because, when we are worried about a negative outcome, we forget that there will also be positive support and resources.

Mission to Power:

1. Set aside time to worry.

Scheduling a designated worry time has been shown to help worriers feel more in control and empowered. Set aside a thirty-minute period on your calendar to think about your problems. To make this most effective, when you catch yourself worrying at any time other than your designated worry time, deliberately think of something else. Then, when it's your time to worry, use it productively. Write out solutions, take actions that you think might ensure a better outcome, and most important, envision positive scenarios that might unfold.

2. Write your worries down.

Writing things down is extremely helpful, especially worries. "Empty" the fears from your mind. Minimize the scary thoughts circling around your head that are causing worry and anxiety. This will tangibly help you reassess the situation you're concerned about.

3. Worry productively.

While you are worrying, you temporarily experience less anxiety because it feels like you are doing something about the problem. However, even though experiencing the fear in your head does distract you from your emotions, it doesn't lead to solutions. The next time you notice you are worrying, do it productively.

For example, if you are worried about mounting bills, consider your options. You could call your creditors to explore different payment arrangements, look for a no-interest credit card to carry you through, make specific plans to decrease future expenses, or consult with a debt advisor. List all the possible solutions or things you can do something about, no matter how insignificant. Focus on what you can change and make an action plan. Write it down to give you relief, otherwise your mind won't think it's real.

4. When a situation is uncertain, stop believing every thought you have about it.

Your mind will naturally create very realistic and detailed scenarios to support your fears, and when you are scared, you forget that your brain lies to you about reality as it rushes to predict the worst-case scenario. When you are traveling down this worry path, it keeps you from enjoying the good things in the present. In moments of worry, force yourself away from believing every negative thought that pops into your head about the outcome. Redirect your energy towards envisioning the result you want to see.

5. Introduce logic.

If you introduce logic to a worrisome situation, your brain will "rethink" what it is thinking, helping to reduce the worry. Whenever you remind yourself to think positively, you emit positive brain waves to counter worry and process situations objectively.

Ask yourself:

– How often has this negative event happened to me in the past?

– How often does this negative event happen to others in this situation?

Let's say you're worried about an important order arriving on time for a big event because you know you are cutting it close. Ask yourself how often you've ordered something and gotten it later than promised. (Is it two times out of ten? Three times out of ten?) How often has the service you used been late? Once you objectively think it through, you'll see that, statistically, the percentage of time you are worrying is greater than the probability that the order will be late, and this will help you scale back your worry naturally.

Affirmations for Strength:

• How I see things is in my mind and in my control.

• I will keep my worry in proportion to the likelihood of the reality.

• I trust that everything will turn out exactly as it should.

PART FOUR

INCREASE YOUR SUPERPOWERS

CHAPTER 6

Gain New Superpowers

The word *superpowers* probably make most of us think of being able to fly, or teleport, or become invisible, like comic book or movie superheroes. While human beings might not have supernatural abilities like those, we do, each of us, have numerous superpowers that define who we are at our deepest level. Once we discover and "own" them, we can use them to navigate life's challenges with greater ease.

Our superpowers have the potential to shape our lives in a positive way and to determine the outcome of our experiences, but we may be out of practice in using them. Or, we may shy away from fully bringing them out, feeling uncertain or insecure. In addition, it's common to emphasize our personal weaknesses, to focus on where we fall short.

This is because our shortfalls get pointed out, first by parents and teachers, and then we point them out ourselves. Unless you were raised in an environment that encouraged you to develop your human superpowers, you might have grown up thinking you don't have any. Rest assured—they are there. Perhaps you just lost touch with them along the way or perhaps you didn't have an opportunity to develop them fully.

Now is a great time to increase the potency of your superpowers or put effort into waking up new ones. Superpowers are like muscles and will strengthen with diligent practice. Naturally, each archetype naturally embodies some superpowers rather than others, but it's wise to practice them all to give you an advantage when dealing with the twists and turns of life.

SUPERPOWERS TO STRENGTHEN

ADAPTABILITY

WHAT: Adaptability is the ability to adjust to new conditions. It's a superpower that, when strong, helps you respond to change positively. The more adaptable you are, the less stress you will experience in any situation. If you have high adaptability, you are better able to go with the flow and be flexible yet calm, in situations where you have no control.

AWARENESS TO EMBRACE: The need for adaptability in life has never been greater than it is now.

The world is changing at a quick pace—from modern technology to unprecedented progress and even unpredictable weather patterns that take us out of our zone of expectation. We update our operating systems and our smartphones regularly, but we forget that we need to update our personal operating systems, as well.

Each of us has a "comfort zone"; the larger it is, the more adaptable we are. A comfort zone is where things are easy for you, where you experience minimal stress. Just outside this zone is the "stretch" zone, a place of some discomfort. By regularly going to the stretch zone, you can expand your comfort zone and grow it in a manageable way.

Develop adaptability by going to the stretch zone often so you can stay calm no matter what is going on around you.

MISSION TO POWER:

1. Practice adaptability in low-stake situations.

Do small, incremental things each day to stretch your comfort zones. Consciously look for opportunities to try new things that will keep you learning. Learn a new skill, try a new food, seek out challenges at work, reinvent yourself, change your hairstyle, drive a new way home, order a different drink, etc.

2. Change your behavior next time you are faced with something unexpected.

Resisting change is natural, but if you decide to embrace it, you will bounce back faster. So, let's say plans change and you feel disappointed. Even if you don't feel like it, respond enthusiastically. If your car breaks down and you can't go where you were planning, accept the new situation and see what good comes of it.

When things happen unexpectedly, decide that it is a good thing, and watch how quickly you adapt to the unexpected.

3. Be the one to come up with solutions.

Research shows that the people who can come up with solutions to a problem are better able to cope with change. The next time you encounter something unexpected, make a list of potential ways to get out of it. This puts you in control and forces your brain to move forward positively instead of shutting down and releasing stress hormones.

4. Decide how adaptability will help you.

If you define what you need to develop more flexibility for, you will be more motivated. For example, if you value relationships, think about how your relationships will specifically improve. Will you get into fewer arguments? Will you have the capacity to be more supportive? If you work in a field that is shrinking due to technology, then envision yourself changing course successfully; this will be a great motivator for learning adaptability. Be specific about how adaptability will help your life, because once you see the benefit, you'll move towards it more eagerly.

CONFIDENCE

WHAT: Confidence is a feeling or belief that you can do something well, that you can succeed at whatever you put your mind to. It's a feeling that arises when you appreciate your own abilities and feel certain that you can rely on yourself. When you are confident, you not only achieve more, you feel happier and more successful.

AWARENESS TO EMBRACE: We are not born with confidence; we develop it.

While it may seem that some people are born confident, the truth is that confidence is not a fixed attribute. It's the result of the thoughts you think and the actions you take. Confidence is not based on your actual ability to succeed at something, but on your *belief* in your ability to succeed.

For example, it's based on your *belief* in your ability to learn something new, your *belief* in your ability to bounce back from a challenge, your *belief* in your ability to start a business or deliver a presentation successfully. The beliefs you hold (whether they are true or not) direct your actions and determine your level of confidence.

Science has shown that building confidence can be done with intent. With consistent effort, you can gradually expand your confidence and rewire your brain for certainty.

MISSION TO POWER:

1. Decide what you want in life.

Start by clearly defining what you truly would love to be, do, and have in your life. Answer these questions:

- What do I want to be?
- What do I want to do?
- What do I want to have?

It doesn't matter whether you are far from what you want, or not. When you know who you are and what you want, your energy level naturally rises and your confidence increases.

2. Determine where you are already confident and where you are not.

You are confident in some areas of your life and not in others. Where do you compare yourself to others and minimize your strengths? Where do you have unrealistic expectations of yourself?

Identify a situation where you felt extremely confident. What was it about that time? Was it what you were doing? Was it the support you had? Was it the people you were with? Was it because you were prepared? Get clear on multiple scenarios so you can tap into the powerful feeling of confidence when you need it.

Next, identify where you lack confidence. When do you get negative about yourself and your abilities? Where do you want to improve your confidence? Get specific. Is it confidence to start a new business, to get an advanced degree, to learn a new skill, to make new friends, to date again, to go on a trip alone to a foreign country?

Make a complete statement: "I want to have more confidence to _____." You can more easily develop confidence when you acknowledge the areas that are important to you. This takes your focus off the void (where you don't have confidence) and puts it on your value (where you want to gain confidence).

3. Decide where you are headed.

Instead of thinking about where you lack confidence or why you weren't confident in the past, refocus your attention. Start affirming who you want to be in the future, and envision scenarios of what you being confident would look like. Start seeing a new reality and you'll more easily move into it when the time comes.

4. Stop comparing yourself to others.

Your confidence immediately drops when you compare yourself unfavorably to others. Your lack of confidence comes from a gap between where you see yourself now and where you think you should be. If you are going to compare yourself, compare yourself to yourself and to your own progress. Monitor your improvement, and see how far you've come. It's important to focus on yourself when it comes to building confidence.

4. Find some personal cheerleaders.

Although confidence is an inner state, you can also boost your confidence by surrounding yourself with people who provide encouragement, positivity, and inspiration and with those who see your greatness. Stop sharing your goals with those who cause you to feel self-doubt by pointing out the negative all the time.

5. Practice confident body language.

When people feel powerful and confident, their body language shows it by adopting more expansive poses. Confident people stand up straighter and literally take up more space. Our postures are an expression of how we feel.

Studies show that we can choose to put ourselves in confident postures, which sends a message to our brain that affects our physiology. So, if you stand in the traditional Superman pose for just two minutes (feet hip-distance apart, shoulders back, chest out, hands on waist with elbows bent), it can increase the dominance hormone testosterone, and decrease the stress hormone cortisol.

The relationships between posture and stress and feeling powerful have been documented, so do this pose often, especially before a situation where you want to feel more confident from within.

CONSIDERATION

WHAT: Consideration means being kindly and thoughtfully concerned about the feelings and situations of others. Being considerate means being able to put yourself in others' shoes and understand what is important to them. When you show consideration, you not only step outside of yourself and show respect, but also positively affirm their value. Practicing consideration means that you actively choose to see beyond what is good for you.

AWARENESS TO EMBRACE: How you treat others is how you invite them to treat you.

Human beings have a core need to be valued. When you treat others with care and consideration, you will notice that, over time, people will reflect this same treatment back to you. This is because relationships function like a mirror, reflecting back to you what you give. We live in a world of balance where energy is always evenly exchanged. Your return might not come in the same form that you give it, and you might not get it back from the same people to whom you are considerate, but the return will be apparent in the bigger picture.

MISSION TO POWER:

1. Remember that people are in your life for a reason.

Nothing happens by accident or chance. Every person you meet has a role in your life. Some will support you, some will hurt you, some will inspire you, and some will help you grow. Remember that this is why you are in others' lives; your paths have crossed for a reason. Keep this topmost in your mind as you go through the day, and be a person who is a positive force in other's lives.

2. Don't judge people by their past.

Everyone has a past. Everyone has a story. Everyone is going through challenges, and everyone has made mistakes. Instead of judging others, support them. How would you like to be treated? Help others move towards what they want in life by your non-judgmentalism and sincere words of support. When you choose to have a more open mind-set, you embrace consideration.

3. Choose kindness no matter what.

It's easy to be kind to people that you like and respect. It's not so easy with those you resent, dislike, or have a negative opinion about. True kindness lies in the act of giving without judging and without expectation of getting something in return. Practice kindness. Challenge people patiently. Try to see things from their point of view. Be kind, even if you don't feel like it.

4. Remember, you are no better than others.

It's easy to get caught up in our own standards of success and look down on those who aren't as successful, accomplished, or as well-educated. However, the reality is that you don't know how far they've come or what they have overcome, or even where they will end up. Be kind and considerate no matter what their situation is.

5. Cultivate perception.

Start observing those you interact with more closely. Read their responses by noticing their expressions, their body language, and their choice of words. If you understand the vibe and nuance of others, you can read them more easily. When you understand people, they will feel more comfortable with you.

6. Anticipate needs.

One way to show ultra-consideration is to anticipate what someone might need. Begin by observing others and getting to know their habits and the circumstances in which you both operate. Whether it's setting up the tables and chairs for the meeting in the right configuration before people arrive, bringing extra pens, or buying water for your travel mates—anytime you can anticipate a need, others will appreciate your consideration.

7. Put yourself in the other person's shoes.

Before you talk to someone about something that is upsetting you, ask yourself if it is the right time for that person to hear what you have to say. Doing this doesn't mean that you change your whole schedule to accommodate them, but if you consider how your words will sound from their perspective, it can help you articulate your message and choose the best time to give it, especially if the person may feel hurt.

8. Be on time.

People who are constantly late send a subtle message to others that they don't value the other person's time. If this is you—even if you are not doing it intentionally, even if showing up late is a habit, and even if you are busy—you come across as inconsiderate. A solution would be to schedule more space between meeting times so that you can arrive on time.

CREATIVITY

WHAT: Creativity is the ability to generate ideas, alternatives, or possibilities or to recognize them when you see them. When you are creative, you see hidden patterns and connections between things that are not normally related and come up with new ways of solving problems and approaching situations.

Creativity is traditionally associated with art, music, writing and dance, but creativity is a skill that is central and useful in all parts of our lives. Most of the things that are interesting and important to us as human beings are the results of creativity. Studies show that when we are involved in creativity or are in a creative state, we are excited and feel that we are living more fully.

AWARENESS TO EMBRACE: Human beings are born creative and then they are taught to be uncreative as they grow older.

Many of us think we aren't creative, but research proves that non-creative behavior is learned over time. In a study, a group of 1,600 five-year-olds was tested for creativity. 98 percent of them tested as creative geniuses, demonstrating that they could think in such innovative ways as Picasso, Einstein, and others known for creative genius. When the group was ten years old, that number had dropped to 30 percent, and by the time they were fifteen years old, the number had dropped to 12 percent. The same test given to 280,000 adults found that only 2 percent were creative geniuses.

Strengthening your creativity muscle helps you find solutions to life challenges with greater ease. Research suggests that creative individuals earn more money, live happier lives, and generate more new ideas across all industries. The best news is that you have creativity within you, you just need to uncover it.

MISSION TO POWER:

1. Stop telling yourself that you aren't creative.

We believe what we say to ourselves, and what we believe shapes our reality. If don't you think you are creative and are always telling yourself or others that you aren't, you won't be able to awaken the creative genius lying dormant within you. What you believe about yourself profoundly affects your capabilities. So, begin affirming that you are creative and that you do have the capability to generate new ideas, and you will remove any psychological barriers that might get in the way.

2. Spend time alone and unplug.

According to one study, 72 percent of people have creative insights and ideas in the shower. This is because doing things alone, such as showering, walking, hiking, driving or daydreaming, gets the brain moving towards a more creative space. Often the best ideas come when you are not actively trying to find them. Creativity is supported when you are unplugged, so make the time to "do nothing" and relax.

3. Get lost in something you love doing.

The time we spend working or taking care of life's obligations doesn't support creativity. To enhance the development of your ability to be creative, your life needs balance. Since love and creativity are intertwined, anything you love doing will help you relax, reduce your stress, and boost your ability to tap into your creativity when you need it.

4. Embrace diversity daily.

People who are creative understand that they can't do the same thing day in and day out and still be creative. They make space for new ideas by doing things that have nothing to do with their profession. Fresh insights come from interacting with a wide range of people and gaining appreciation of broader perspectives than your own. Spend time in different places, with different people. Pursue new experiences, and challenge yourself to see people and places with a new set of eyes.

5. Travel with a new intent.

Practice "active" travel. When you travel, instead of just visiting landmarks, sightseeing, and finding good food to eat, make it a point to take an interest in the people and the culture of the locale. A study on creativity showed that how we think about the world and people affects our creative ability. When you travel, you have the opportunity to see a larger perspective and move away from your habitual thinking, and that stimulates your creative thinking processes. So, the next time you travel, make it "active" travel.

CURIOSITY

WHAT: Curiosity is a key ingredient of learning. Not only does it lead to increased knowledge, but it also stimulates the ability to make connections between various pieces of information, and that is what helps us survive. The urge to explore and find new things helps us to stay relevant and in synch with our constantly changing environment.

AWARENESS TO EMBRACE: Curiosity boosts other superpowers and enhances success in life.

Research shows that curiosity is the fuel that supports other superpowers, such as creativity, positivity, and adaptability. When you choose to be more curious, you not only increase your energy and enthusiasm for life, but your memory improves. Over two hundred studies have found that conscientious curiosity has as much of an impact on achievement and success in life as intelligence.

We are all curious as children. As we grow older and begin to develop fixed goals and concrete interests, we lose our sense of curiosity—to the point that only a bare minimum remains within the average adult.

Being curious opens you up to new ideas and novel solutions. It also fosters perseverance. Many geniuses, such as Einstein, Galileo, and Leonardo da Vinci, were documented as being extraordinarily curious and inquisitive.

MISSION TO POWER:

1. Practice being extremely open-minded toward anything new.

Bias decreases curiosity, so when you are faced with anything—whether a question, a task, or a challenging situation—remind yourself to stay open and curious about how to proceed. The minute you think you know the answer or that there is only one way to handle it, you shut down your ability to discover a new way and potentially better way to move forward.

2. Ask questions.

We often take things for granted. We don't think to question something that's been presented to us, but when you ask questions, you not only gather new information, but you also identify your knowledge gaps and begin to think creatively. Ask questions like: What is that? Why is it done that way? Who made that rule? How does it work?

3. Avoid boredom and routine.

The number-one enemy of curiosity is routine. When you are in a routine or stuck in a rut, you are doing the same thing, day after day. This leads to boredom. Boredom happens when you aren't interested, and you aren't being stimulated. To avoid boredom, change up your routines. It can be as simple as brushing your teeth with the opposite hand for one week, moving the trash to a different part of the room, exploring a new route for your morning commute, or checking out a new type of exercise.

4. Diversify your life portfolio.

If you always listen to pop music, try listening to classical. If you always watch Discovery Channel try National Geographic. If you like cooking chicken, try duck. The most brilliant people in the world have diverse backgrounds. They've tried everything and have many experiences. New experiences keep your mind active and curious.

5. Listen without judgment.

It's easy to make assumptions as we listen to others, and to form opinions without first seeking to understand the other's perspective. Next time you are talking to someone, especially someone you don't always see eye to eye with, practice listening without judging them or being invested in the outcome. Ask questions to get more clarity and understanding.

FOCUS

WHAT: Focus is a skill that helps you to fix your attention on a task without distraction or procrastination until the task is complete. Focus is what helps you concentrate on what you need to do, even amidst distractions and setbacks, so that you can sustain your effort and energy until you reach your goal.

AWARENESS TO EMBRACE: The inability to focus when we are not inspired by a task comes from a need to escape.

When you are doing something you don't really feel like doing, your brain perceives it as a threat and grabs any opportunity to escape. The "opportunity" (distraction) could be a sound, a random thought, or a sudden need. Even if you are doing something of tantamount importance, your brain doesn't want you to miss anything, and because of this, you find yourself unable to concentrate on the task at hand.

We have a misconception that we have difficulty focusing or that we can't focus. Really, though, we have trouble deciding. For example, when we have a hard deadline, we focus easily until the task is done because the deadline does the deciding for us. The secret to being able to focus "better" is not to "try harder;" it's to remove as many distractions as you can and make some decisions.

MISSION TO POWER:

1. At the beginning of the day (or week), make two lists.

If you tend to multitask, jumping from one thing to another, this is a great way to make decisions and commit to getting things done. On the first list, write down everything that you need to accomplish that day. Circle your top five "must dos" and write them on a separate piece of paper.

You now have your second list, your "A List." Anything you didn't circle is what you must avoid at all costs. No matter what, you can't do anything until you accomplish your A List. This works because it forces you to make a hard decision and eliminate anything that is not the best use of your time.

2. Choose one priority task.

Decide at the beginning of the day something that you must get done by the end of the day, no matter what. It's non-negotiable. Even if you will do other things throughout the day, this is the one thing that you commit to getting done. The power of this strategy lies in the way it forces you to organize yourself around a priority.

3. Plan ahead to focus.

Use sleep to do your work for you. Research has found that our brains go through our day when we are sleeping to create memories. It transfers information from our short-term memory to our long-term memory and organizes our thoughts.

At the end of your current day, plan what you want to do the next day. If you tell your brain the day before what the next day looks like, it will help you focus.

4. Make sure you take breaks.

Attention is a limited resource. The more you focus, the harder it is to focus and the less able you are to focus. To counter this, plan to take breaks. Do chunks of highly focused sessions, and then take a break. Make sure you don't deplete yourself because, if you do, focus will be elusive for a while.

When you take your break, do something completely different. If you were on your computer, mingle with people, and vice-versa. Different activities stimulate different neurons. Another good tactic is to let your mind wander without judgment. A short nap will reset your reserve, too. The idea is to take breaks after periods of high focus and concentration.

5. Schedule energy-consuming tasks at the right time.

We all vary in that our energy is greatest at different times of the day. Anything that requires your full attention should be scheduled at a time of day when you actually have energy to focus. If you are a morning person, schedule challenging tasks in the morning. If you are more energetic in the late afternoon, then plan your most challenging work at that time of day.

6. Take a forced technology break.

Since focus is about getting rid of distractions, determine your biggest distractions and turn them off or put them somewhere else. Email is usually a big distraction for people when working at a desk, but you can decide to put what's important to you first instead of what's important to others first. Like email. Don't check email until the time that you have pre-decided.

The phone is another distraction. Researchers found in 2017 that it didn't matter whether a person's smartphone was turned on or off, or whether it was lying face-up or face-down on a desk. If it was within sight or easy reach, it reduced people's ability to focus because part of their brains was actively working to keep from picking up or looking at the phone. The solution is to leave your phone in another room when you are trying to focus.

7. Write down distracting thoughts to clear them from your mind.

If you start to do one thing and get distracted by thoughts of other things you need to do, use a To Do list as an external memory device. While helping to settle your mind by assuring that you won't forget something important, it will help you prioritize and stay on track.

INTUITION

WHAT: Intuition is the ability to understand something without the need for conscious reasoning. Some people think of intuition as a mystical power, whereas skeptics pass it off as lucky guesswork. However, scientists who study the phenomenon say that intuition is a very real ability and that they can identify intuition on brain scans and lab experiments.

AWARENESS TO EMBRACE: Your intuition is an "inner voice" that knows more than your rational logic will allow.

You've probably had moments when you felt that something wasn't quite right. You didn't know why you felt that way, and yet you did. It's easy to dismiss intuitive flashes because often they don't seem to make sense, especially because as a culture, we've learned to believe that logic is reality. However, the "feeling" that comes from within is something that can provide beneficial insight in situations where considering both intuition and logic will help you make the best decision.

Studies show that the human heart encompasses a degree of intelligence that can be cultivated to our advantage. The ability to create positive states within ourselves provides the doorway for opening our intuition because, when we are feeling calm and peaceful, that is when intuitional insights start to flow. Intuition can be developed and strengthened with practice.

MISSION TO POWER:

1. Become observant of your energy.

Really pay attention to how you feel when you are with others. Who makes you feel tired and drained? Who makes you feel energetic and inspired? Note those you don't feel your best around without judging it as right or wrong. This is your intuition telling you that you are losing energy to someone. We may feel bad about it if it's someone we think we should like or support. Start by simply observing and noting it.

2. Recognize your form of intuition.

If you want to develop and use your intuition, it is important to recognize it when it speaks to you. Intuition is soft and subtle, and if you are not paying attention, you might miss it. Is your form of intuition visual? That is, do you "see" images in your mind? Do you see things in quick flashes? Or is it a "feeling," a hunch? Does it come as a thought? Or do you hear words in your head?

Sometimes intuition is felt as a physical sensation, what we call "chicken skin" or "goose bumps" when something feels right or, for example, a clenching of your stomach when something doesn't feel right. Your intuition may show up as a deep sense of knowing and certainty. If you can remember how it felt when you knew something to be true deep in your heart, tune into that feeling and use it as a guide.

No matter what the form, when you need clarity, set an intention before the event to listen with both you mind and your heart (intuition) and note the sensations you get during and after. This will strengthen your intuition.

3. Be aware of your intuitive sight.

Your eyes see far more than you realize, as there are things you don't see consciously, but you see intuitively. It's been scientifically documented that we have two vision tracks, one conscious and the other intuitive. Our intuitive vision track operates even when we aren't aware of it, constantly receiving visual stimuli.

Therefore, if you find you are in a situation that makes you feel nervous seemingly for "no reason," it may be that your intuitive insight has picked up something and found a reason to be concerned. Pay attention to what you feel; don't shrug it off as nothing.

4. Make it a point to notice your heart's response.

Make a habit of noting what your heart says and the way you feel in response to everything that happens to you. It's hard to lead with your intuition when you have been programmed that using your brain is the "smart" way to operate. The human brain's rational capacities are far more error-prone than our intuition. That's why the answer you think is "the best" may not be. The reality is that complex problems for which you can't find a logical answer are best solved by leading with your intuitive capacities. It's a life-affirming practice to acknowledge your heart in every situation, so that when you need another perspective, it's there for you.

5. Do three minutes of meditation.

Studies show that just three minutes of mindful, intentional, quiet time a day can get you more in touch with your intuition. Take yourself away from other people by going for a walk, being out in nature, or just sitting with yourself. Take note of how you feel. Assess your energy level. Get in tune with yourself by acknowledging your state without judging yourself.

6. Practice to develop your intuition.

Try the following technique to shift your emotional state and send positive emotions through your system, which will help you connect to your intuition. Do this a few times a day.

- Close your eyes and shift your attention to the area around your heart. Breathe slowly and deeply.

- Keeping your focus on the heart area, intentionally breathe in for five seconds and then breathe out for five seconds. Do this a few times.

- Think of someone you love and cherish. Activate the genuine feeling of care and appreciation you have for them by thinking about them. Focus on how good it feels as you continue to breathe with your focus on the area of your heart.

7. Use sleep to tune in to your intuition.

The REM stage of sleep is great for problem solving and gaining clarity on uncertain situations. You receive insights that you wouldn't get when you are awake, and because they activate the emotional area of the brain, the things that are most important to you are prioritized and "worked through." Solutions to problems and aha! moments have been shown to come following REM sleep. Our dreams help us to get unstuck from our logical, daytime mind-set.

You can use sleep to strengthen your intuition. Before you go to sleep, think about or write down a problem to which you need a solution. Set an intention that your intuitive solution will emerge the following day.

LISTENING SKILLS

WHAT: Being a good listener is more than just hearing what another person says. A good listener takes in what the other is saying, sometimes deeply. A good listener reads between the lines, asks questions, and offers support without giving suggestions, letting her attention drift, or judging. Being a good listener means that you don't try to fix the other's problem; instead, you tune in to their feelings and stay present with them.

AWARENESS TO EMBRACE: Good listening skills have advantages in three distinct areas of your life.

Practical: Having good listening skills is, of course, practical. They connect you to what's going on around you and with others, and they help you understand your responsibilities and decide which actions to take for your personal success.

Social bonding: Good listening skills are important socially. In any relationship, professional or personal, there is no relationship if one person is not listening and relating to the other. Good listening skills help people feel supported and connected to you.

Growth: All of us have a world of our own containing our thoughts, ideas, opinions, and perspectives. We don't learn things from what we have to say to others; but we learn from what others say to us. When you listen without internal judgment and are truly open, you expand your mind and perspective.

MISSION TO POWER:

1. Remove distractions.

Put your cell phone on silent and out of sight. Turn off sounds such as email notifications. Turn off the television or any other device that could be distracting. Studies show that even having your cell phone off is distracting if it is still in sight. You may think you're listening, but part of your focus stays on the phone if you can see it.

2. Practice being mindful.

While we all know it's rude to pick up your phone and check your emails while someone is talking (even though you may want to), internal distractions are a lot harder to avoid. If you're mindful, you are focusing on what the other person is saying instead of thinking about whether you agree or what you have to do later in the day. When this happens, catch yourself and gently direct your attention back to the speaker. Become curious about what she has to say. People can sense when you've tuned out.

3. Refrain from interrupting or changing the subject.

A good listener lets the other person complete a thought without interruption. Remember, you are not there to share your expertise unless asked. As a listener, listen. If you interrupt, the person may feel that you are only interested in talking about yourself, or worse, feel that you haven't heard what they are saying.

4. Practice mirroring.

A great strategy for active listening is to mirror the person you are in conversation with. Without mimicking them exactly, reflect back to them the same tone, pace, gestures, and body language. This helps you build rapport and makes the other person feel safe and comfortable. You can also summarize what you've heard, further reinforcing that you are listening and understand their point of view.

5. Be comfortable with a pause before speaking.

Usually, we are busy formulating our response when the other person is talking. When you notice that you are doing this, stop and listen. Allow a space of silence in the conversation. When there is space, it allows the person you're speaking with a place to add in more of what they are thinking and feeling. Even if the silent space is uncomfortable for you, push past the discomfort. Sometimes connection is felt in that silent space.

6. Watch for body language cues.

We may think we communicate through words, but our expressions, body language, and tone of voice say volumes. Watch the person you are speaking with carefully. Does he say that everything's great when his face doesn't reflect that? Does she say she is open but have her arms crossed? When you read what others are saying beyond their words, it may lead you to respond to their actual state.

7. Be curious and ask questions.

Questions help people uncover solutions they might not otherwise have thought of. Open-ended questions that require more than a yes or no invite deeper insight. As well, asking a question as a follow-up to a comment shows the other person you are engaged. Listen more than you question. Something as simple as, "Can you tell me more about that?" is enough to show you are really listening.

PATIENCE

WHAT: Patience is the capacity to accept delays, challenges, or hardships without losing energy or focus by getting annoyed or frustrated. It's considered a virtue, yet you don't have to be born with it; it's a skill, and it can be strengthened. The more patience you have, the greater your emotional freedom. Another way to look at patience is to think of it as your level of endurance before negativity takes over.

AWARENESS TO EMBRACE: There are proven wellness benefits to being patient.

These facts are backed by university research studies published between 2013 - 2015:

- The more patience you have, the better decision maker you tend to be.

- The more patience you have, the better you can work with others.

- The more patient you are, the less you tend to procrastinate.

- The more patient you are, the less depression and fewer negative feelings you experience.

- The more patient you are, the calmer your mind and the more gratitude you feel for life.

- The more patient you are, the less likely you are to experience ulcers and headaches.

Patience is a key you can use to unlock greater potential and to have a more fulfilling life.

MISSION TO POWER

1. Make yourself wait.

Instant gratification is so satisfying. Getting what you want right away seems the best thing that could happen. However, research shows that waiting for things makes us happier in the long run, and the way to get into the habit of waiting is to practice.

Start small: Delay checking your phone for messages for ten minutes when you don't have to. Wait ten minutes before reaching for a snack once you are aware you want one. Delay ordering something online that you want but don't need. Conscious daily practice of delaying gratification will start spilling over into other irritating situations, and you'll discover you have more patience to apply.

2. Embrace being uncomfortable.

Anything outside our comfort zone makes us impatient because it's human nature to want to be comfortable. This means you can cultivate patience by getting comfortable with the uncomfortable. When you begin to feel impatient, affirm to yourself, "This is simply uncomfortable, not intolerable."

3. Take a few deep breaths.

We all know that we should breathe when we feel upset or impatient, but how often do we remember to do it? Let this be a reminder. Use breathing as a tool to calm your mind and body. All you need to do is take a few big deep breaths and watch how your tension melts away.

4. Be mindful of what's making you impatient.

Our lives are filled with places to go, things to do, and goals to fulfill. All of this occupies space in our brains, and our minds jump from task to task and thought to thought. When something like traffic slows us down or a slow register line threatens to make us late, we automatically jump to frustration, impatient to get where we need to go. At times like this, ask yourself, "Have I gotten caught up in the hurry? Is this slowdown a reminder to stay more present?"

5. Change your perception of time.

We say to others all the time, "There's just not enough time in the day!" or "I don't ever have the time to..." We affirm a lack of time or a speed of time so often that we create that exact reality for ourselves. So, when something doesn't happen in a timely manner, we get impatient.

Time expands and contracts according to your mental attitude. While it's true that you have all the time you need for everything in your life, if you continue to affirm the lack of time, you will trigger impatience and get upset with every delay.

POSITIVITY

WHAT: Positivity is the experience of pleasant emotions, most commonly described as joy, serenity, pride, amusement, love, inspiration, awe, hope, interest, and gratitude. Positivity is difficult to maintain because we human beings have a natural bias toward negativity. Given that we can't avoid negative events in life, if you want to experience more positivity, you will need to work on making sure that your life has a greater positive to negative ratio.

AWARENESS TO EMBRACE: Positivity is not *only* about focusing on the positive, as many think.

Many people think that being positive means to look at the good side of things and ignore everything else, when in fact, trying too hard to be positive can trigger a proportionately opposite amount of negativity. The harder you try to be happy, upbeat, and positive, the more you will tend to feel sad, down, and negative. This is because both positive and negative exist in our experience of life. So, people who are the most positive recognize that life has both sides, and they choose to focus their energy and time on the side that's going to promote the best outcome.

MISSION TO ACTION:

1. Make it a priority to overcome the negativity bias.

Our negativity bias causes us to feel our negative emotions more intensely than our positive emotions. Because of this, we pay more attention to negative stories and remember negative events more easily. Research shows that we typically recall four negative memories for every positive one.

Your personal positivity ratio can be improved upon if you consistently notice what's good, specifically, about situations you are in. You can strengthen this through random acts of kindness, offering words of appreciation for others or actively adding a few more positive thoughts to your day. Any other positivity-inducing activity or focus will help, such as those listed below. The benefits of positivity occur when our perceived ratio of positive-to-negative emotions is at least three positives to one negative.

2. Start your day off in a positive way.

The way you begin your day sets the tone for how the rest of the day unfolds, so make a point to start it well. When you wake up, do some deep breathing and focus on the good things about your day (even if you know it's going to be challenging).

Read something inspiring, have uplifting conversations with those you live with (if you can). Create a ritual that you can depend on, one that you feel good about, even if it means waking up before everyone else so you have "your time."

3. Practice appreciation and gratitude.

This works. It's one of the fastest ways to shift your focus away from the challenges of disappointment, negativity, and judgment. Get a notebook and label it your Gratitude journal. In it, list the things for which you are truly thankful, and be specific. Instead of just writing, "I'm thankful for my friends," write the name of the friend and what specific action or quality you appreciate. Nothing is too minimal to list. Doing this daily is a wonderful way to move toward more positivity. This practice can cause a noticeable and immediate shift in your perspective, as it lifts your energy and brings more into your life to be thankful for.

4. Make your home a place you enjoy being.

Even if you have no control over the state of the paint and carpet, you do have control over what you put on your walls, what you surround yourself with, and how tidy you keep it. Place inspirational images around you, dedicate a shelf or an area to belongings that are important to you, and make your environment a place that you come home to. A space where you feel welcomed can add a lot of positivity to your life.

5. Lift your body to lift your energy.

Your mind and body have an intrinsic connection. Each impacts the other. If you close your eyes and think of sucking on a lemon wedge, your mouth will water. In the same way, if you are struggling to move your thoughts into a more positive perspective, move your body there first.

Stand up straight, put your shoulders back, and stretch your arms out as far as you can go. Mindful walking with "positive posture" will influence your mind to move towards positivity, as well.

6. Surround yourself with more of the positive.

It's hard to maintain a positive perspective if you are constantly pulled down by the negativity of those around you. If you get caught up in a negative conversation, gracefully steer the conversation in a better direction. If you are always surrounded by negative people, this may be a good time to reevaluate those with whom you spend time.

Who are the three most negative people you spend time with? Plan a way to minimize that time. What are the three most negative sources of information you spend time on? Substitute them with something more positive.

7. Self-monitor your thoughts.

When challenges happen, it's easy to lose perspective, especially if you are already stressed and moving too fast, and something that's not a big deal can turn into a huge and insurmountable obstacle in your mind. Next time something comes up that throws your thoughts into a tailspin, do this:

Stop: Say "Stop" to yourself, in your mind or out loud. It doesn't matter which. Just catch yourself when negative thoughts start to spiral and before you act on them. Say it over and over to create a break.

Breathe: Sit down, if you can, and focus on your breath as it goes in and out of your body. Do this for a few minutes to center yourself.

Question: What is the next best step to take? Do you need to call someone? Vent? Get advice? Figure out the next best step. Now ask yourself whether, in a day, a week, or a year, this will matter. It's helpful to gain perspective by looking at the bigger picture.

Recall: Remember that, somehow, things work out. Think of a time when you had a challenge that seemed insurmountable, yet somehow, circumstances came together and you got through it. Focus on how things have turned out for you in the past and avoid thinking of worst-case scenarios.

8. Sleep, eat well, and move your body.

This is obvious, but worth taking note of. If you want to be more positive in your mind, you must treat your body well, as your mind and body are intrinsically connected. If you don't treat your body well, you won't feel good, and that makes it very difficult to entertain good thoughts or exude positivity. When you feel better, you'll think more clearly and optimistically. These basic habits have a huge effect on your mindset.

9. Do something kind for someone.

It's easy to get caught up in our own lives and problems, so make it a point to look around and see how you can help someone else. This can provide new and inspiring perspectives and fill your heart with good feelings. Doing something nice can be as simple as making a call just to say hi, helping someone complete a task, complimenting a stranger, or paying it forward by paying for the coffee of a stranger in front of you.

RESILIENCE

WHAT: Resilience is the ability to overcome setbacks with relative ease, to grow from adversity, and to turn potentially negative events into positive ones. Resilient people operate from greater positivity and optimism, which helps to fuel ideas, solve problems, and generally be more effective at whatever they are doing. Although emotional resilience is partially inborn, it is a skill that you can learn and develop. Without it, you are more apt to suffer from burnout, fatigue, depression, defensiveness, and cynicism.

AWARENESS TO EMBRACE: Resilience has a lot to do with perspective.

Neuroscientists have found that we can make ourselves either more or less vulnerable by how we think about challenging situations. If you reframe them in positive terms, even if your initial response was negative, your ability to handle the challenge will change. The more you change your perspective to be more positive, the more lasting the results, and the better you will feel.

MISSION TO ACTION:

1. Do not downplay your struggle or challenges.

Everyone responds differently to challenges, and different things stress people out. Whatever is hard for you, accept that it is valid. Do not compare yourself to anyone else and how they would handle the situation.

2. Notice the ways in which you are already resilient.

You may not have gone through extreme abuse or dealt with homelessness, but you have been through something. Think back to the three toughest times in your life. How did you get through them? Acknowledge the areas within you in which you have resilience. Know your strengths and use them.

3. Learn from the past and question how you are benefitting in the present.

When we have a negative experience, it's easier to blame and complain and find reasons for why it happened than it is to focus on the positive lessons that you can mine from the challenge. However, to become more resilient is to become aware of how challenges help us to grow.

When you have a hard situation, focus on the benefits of that situation. Instead of asking "Why did this happen *to* me?" Ask, "How did this happen *for* me?"

4. Reach out for help.

One of the biggest indicators of how well one copes after a challenge is having people around who cared during the crisis. Build resilience by seeking support from those you trust. It doesn't have to be professional support; it can be a friend or a spouse. When you're going through a hard time, don't withdraw from other people. Accept help from those who care about you.

5. Learn how to take a mental break, and do it often.

While you may not be able to fix the problem that is challenging you, you can protect yourself from getting overwhelmed by taking breaks. Take control and get away. Read a book, hang out with friends, or silence your phone and your computer alerts.

6. Laugh whenever you can.

If you have a sense of humor and look for situations to make you laugh, you will increase your immunity to life's frustrations. Those who have a sense of humor, especially about life's common challenges, experience life as less stressful and are more resilient.

PART FIVE

LIFE TOOLS

CHAPTER 7

Superhero Mind-Set Powers

Your life is one hundred percent your creation. Where you are today was created by every thought you've had and every choice you've made, and you are exactly where you are because of this. Life is not something that happens to you; it's something you create. If you think your life is out of control, it's only because you've chosen to surrender control.

As you go through your life, it's your mindset that brings the situations and circumstances into your path to either support you or challenge you. How you think about what happens and how you see your life make a difference in how you feel and what you are able to powerfully manifest.

Although at times you may doubt it, you actually have everything within you to make your life whatever you want it to be. To enhance your personal power, you can intentionally shift your energetic vibration by integrating the super-virtues of gratitude, appreciation, humility, perspective, spirituality, responsibility, and mindfulness into your daily intentions. When you do so, your life will naturally move towards greater achievement and success in all the areas that are most important to you.

The Power of Appreciation

As human beings, we want to be valued for who we are and recognized for our contributions and accomplishments. A core desire and the most deeply held value of human nature is a need to be appreciated. We want to know that we have made a difference in someone's life. We want to be valued.

When you begin to help others feel valued, simply by being genuinely appreciative of their time, energy, input, and resources, you move into greater power. When you value others, you draw unprecedented value into your own life. You are the key that can unlock the door to goodness and grace, not just for others, but for yourself as well.

It's important to remember that while you are appreciating others, it's also important to include yourself in this practice. After all, you are the most important person in your life, and appreciation of self is the balance to appreciating others.

It's important to remember that if you give abundantly of your time, energy, and resources without feeling appreciated, you will build resentment over time. If you find yourself in this situation, you may think that something is wrong with the other person, when in fact, you are subconsciously upset with yourself for not valuing your time and energy more. Take responsibility for yourself and show appreciation for yourself by reallocating your energy.

Take your appreciation one step further and appreciate what you have in your life. It's easy to focus on what you don't have. While there is nothing wrong with wanting more, if you make it a point to appreciate what you do have and what *is* good in your life, you'll draw more into your life to appreciate.

DAILY MISSION: Appreciate yourself, appreciate others, and appreciate the good you have in your life today. Be specific as to exactly what you appreciate.

The Power of Attitude

What attitude do you take with you as you leave your house in the morning? As you go into a meeting? You probably don't think about it; most people don't have a high level of attitude awareness. Yet being aware of your attitude is important because that's what governs how you perceive the world and how the world perceives you.

Attitude reveals the way you look at life and the way you choose to see and respond to everything that happens around you. Your attitude isn't something that just "happens"; it's something you choose, whether or not you are aware that you are choosing it. Your thoughts control your attitude. You can optimize your life by becoming aware of your thoughts about situations that are especially challenging. Studies have proved that attitude is a better predictor of your success than your IQ.

This doesn't mean you have to be "happy" or upbeat about all situations, but it does mean becoming mindful of your attitude; for example, whether you are looking at what's coming toward you as a positive or a negative. Studies show that, when all other factors are equal, the person with the better attitude wins, advances, or gets more of what they want.

If you notice you have a bad attitude towards certain people, situations, or events, it's likely the product of past experiences. Everyone comes upon hard times, heartache, physical pain, unmet expectations, hurt feelings, and more. It doesn't matter what has happened to you; what matters is how you respond. It takes time and energy to shift your attitude, but the rewards are far reaching. It all begins with awareness.

DAILY MISSION: Be attitudinally self-aware. Consciously choose to adopt a more positive attitude towards any situation you find you feel negative about.

The Power of Divine Timing

We live in an era of instant gratification. If we know what we want, we can find it online in a few seconds. Technology is advancing so rapidly that it's "spoiled" us in terms of convenience, thus cultivating our impatience about what we want to see happen for us.

Anytime something doesn't happen in the timeframe that you desire (or in the way that you desire), it can be incredibly frustrating. You might lose hope and feel down about your life, or even resort to forcing a direction that brings forth undesirable results.

When what you want is "not happening" in your life, make the effort look at it differently. See it from the point of view that what you desire is coming together for you in ways that are not yet apparent. During this lag time, to make the best of it, remind yourself often how much goes on behind the scenes to bring what you want into reality.

The next time you are frustrated that things are happening too slowly, make a conscious note of what *is* happening. Notice what you actually *do* experience each day and appreciate the time it took to manifest. When things finally start happening for you, you'll see that it all really did happen in perfect timing.

Sometimes, when what you want is not manifesting, it's because the direction is not right. Your delays and challenges are simply fate, saving you from something that is all wrong for you. That's because a bigger plan is diverting you from the direction you wanted, so that you can move to toward something better.

Relax into life's flow. When you can do that, you will enjoy the process of life more. Point yourself in the direction you want, all while staying connected to the knowing that everything in your life is unfolding to your ultimate advantage. Trust in the force of life that is moving every aspect of reality to its next best expression.

DAILY MISSION: Focus on the blessings in your life and marvel at the wisdom in the Universe that brought it to you at the right time. Trust that everything that happens is for your highest good, even if it doesn't feel like it.

The Power of Gratitude

While appreciation at its core is about sensing value, gratitude is about expressing your appreciation of that value. Gratitude is a feeling you can cultivate through focused attention on what is good, and it is an emotion that comes from deep within. Practicing gratitude truly can change your life.

If you are grateful, you'll see that more is given to you. If you are not, you'll find that more is taken away. Even if there are things in your life that you don't feel thankful for and wish did not exist, your best bet to get more of the "good" is to sharpen your focus and master your thoughts. Always look for the upside. Just like a friend whose gift you did not show you were thankful for, why would the Universe give you more gifts when you don't seem thankful for the gifts you already have been given?

It is a good practice to find things to be thankful for every day, and not just for the good things, but for all things. What makes who you are today is all that your life has brought you—the highs and lows, pleasure and pain, and happiness and sadness you've experienced along the way.

If you can cultivate the habit of being grateful for every good thing that comes to you, as well as for every undesirable challenge, you will find power. Since *all* things in your life contribute to your advancement and growth, the secret is to include everything as you reflect on what you are grateful for.

DAILY MISSION: Commit to practicing gratitude consistently, day and night. As the practice gains momentum over time, you'll reach a breakthrough. Make sure you are specific when you practice.

The Power of Humility

Humility is about emotional neutrality. You operate without a need to put yourself above others, no matter how much you've achieved. Yet, you do not see yourself as below them no matter how little you've achieved. Humility is the opposite of operating from your ego, where you see yourself as better than or "above" others because of your need to feel special or superior to them. Humility is a mindset that supports seeing yourself as just as valuable, yet no *more* valuable, than any other human being on the planet.

The practice of humility is an essential daily exercise. Although some may think of humility as weak, it's actually an exceptionally strong power. When you show humility, you inspire silent respect from others. Humility not only fosters personal growth, but it keeps your ego from over-reacting, which prevents arguments and curbs your tendency to be defensive.

Anyone who is impressed with their own success and importance stops being impressive, no matter how successful they are. When you consciously and intentionally embrace humility, you remind yourself that you still have a lot to learn. And it's interesting to ponder that, no matter how much you think you know, when compared to the magnificence of the Universe we live in, what you know is really only a drop. If you can be your best, yet let go of the desire to be better than everyone else, your humility will carry you a very long way.

When you can operate with the knowledge that the world doesn't revolve around you, when you are able to withhold your judgment of others and work towards helping others grow and succeed, you can affirm that you've embraced the essence of humility.

You are not in this world to live up to others' expectations, nor are others here to live up to yours. You are here to love others, not judge or fix them, and by embracing this fully, you liberate yourself from ego and are able to more easily act from a place of humility.

DAILY MISSION: Humility can be practiced daily in every situation and interaction. Listen intently to others and put yourself in their shoes when they are talking. Remind yourself that you don't know everything, so question with sincere curiosity, and most important, stop comparing yourself to others.

The Power of Mindfulness

We live our days with wandering minds. For example, have you ever drifted off in thought while reading a book and been halfway through a page before you realized you weren't absorbing what you read? Have you ever driven home but not remembered the details of the journey or pet your dog while thinking of other things? Research shows that our minds wander 47 percent of the time. That's almost half our lives that we have been missing because we are not present!

Because our repeated experiences shape our brain and sculpt our experiences, paying attention to what we are doing is good, but *how* we pay attention is the important part of mindfulness that is often misunderstood. Mindfulness is not just about being present and aware; it's also about not judging where you are and accepting your state of mind—as well as the moment.

You can "be friends" with any moment you are in, no matter whether it's painful or frightening. Instead of feeling like you can't do anything until this thing that you don't like has passed, you feel at peace with it internally. If you are not at peace with it, your inner experience is driven by liking or hating the moment. Spaciousness of mind comes through accepting any moment. If you practice mindfulness, you can be amidst tremendous challenges and simultaneously have immense composure and clarity because you are less emotionally reactive.

DAILY MISSION: More than a state of mind, mindfulness is a way of being. Bring your awareness to any state you are in. If you are irritated or confused, practice being "okay" with it. If you are happy elated and joyful, practice being "okay" with that.

The Power of Perspective

Being able to reframe challenging situations to your advantage is a powerful skill that can transform your life experiences and help you to rise above anything that brings you down emotionally. It allows you to see through anything that traps you mentally. It allows you to gain vision and keeps you centered. Perspective helps you to find solutions and pursue opportunities that you wouldn't find if you kept a limited perspective. When you intentionally notice what you haven't noticed before, you open yourself up to unprecedented possibilities.

Have you ever gone into your kitchen and noticed the clean dishes instead of the dirty dishes? Don't we usually focus on the "negative" of the dirty dishes and, if there are a lot, feel upset. However, what if you went into your kitchen and noticed the clean dishes first—the dirty dishes would still be there, but they would seem minimal in proportion. When "dirty" is not the main focus, you're likely to be less upset.

Another analogy on perspective is the classic half-full, half-empty glass example. Rather than seeing the glass as half-empty or half-full, what if you simply saw a glass on the table with water in it? This perspective would open you up to notice that there is a pitcher filled with water on the counter so that you can refill the glass when you run out. When you change perspective, you see things in their entirety, and that works to your advantage.

With the uncertainty and challenges we face in life, the outcome depends on your perspective, and that in turn will drive your choices. What we see depends on what we are looking for. Develop the ability to reframe situations, as this will profoundly affect your life and how you relate to others.

DAILY MISSION: In every situation, consciously choose to look for the objective perspective. Look at it from the other person's perspective. Go into the future and look back and see it from the perspective of time passing. Look at it from a non-judgmental perspective. Consider every angle.

The Power of Responsibility

You alone are responsible for your life. It takes courage to embrace this truth, but it's the only way to turn away from thinking that life happens *to* you to understanding that life happens *for* you, and being able to attract what you want into your life. The moment you accept that you are responsible for everything that happens—both the good and the not so good—life becomes a gift that unfolds in incredible ways.

We all know that we are responsible for ourselves, but you may not fully accept that you are also responsible for everything that happens along your path of life. Start taking responsibility for it by not blaming your problems on the people or situations around you. Accept where you are, see the benefits of the challenges, and ask yourself what you want and how you can fulfill it. The moment you accept responsibility, you become a magnet for opportunities, as people and positive energy are irresistibly drawn towards confidence, clarity, inspiration, and certainty.

When challenges happen or when things don't go as planned, instead of blaming others or making excuses, see it as the Universe looking out for you. Maybe you need to be stronger and better prepared for something coming up in your life and need to be shaken up to see a different perspective or you need to move on to a new and better path.

DAILY MISSION: Accept personal responsibility for everything going on in your life. No matter what challenge you experience, take responsibility by seeing it as a gift and finding the benefits, even though you might not see the value until some time has passed.

The Power of Reflection

Every person in your life and every situation you encounter offer opportunities to grow through the power of reflection. People will treat you exactly the same way as you unconsciously treat yourself. If you see value within yourself, the world will treat you in like manner.

For example, whenever someone doesn't appreciate the value of your time and it's bothering you, ask yourself where you fail to appreciate the value of your own time. Similarly, when you feel slighted by a cutting remark, ask yourself in what way you have been cutting yourself down.

Take control of your daily experiences by being consciously aware of the beliefs and feelings you have about you, and then monitor them as people reflect them. As you begin to treat yourself better, you can transform your experience of how others treat you.

The Law of Reflection says that you have whatever qualities you see in others. If a particular person stresses you out, it's helpful to ask yourself whether *you* may be perceived as a source of someone else's stress.

Since many of our stressful situations involve other people, it's wise to think twice about our judgments. We create stress from a place of ego and exaggerate our judgments. When we take time to reflect and see that we do similar things, we find center. The more you reflect, the more realistic your expectations of others will be and the less stress you will accumulate.

DAILY MISSION: What can you focus on within yourself every single day to create a shift in your life? Remember, it all starts with you and what you choose to focus on.

The Power of Spirituality

Spirituality can be defined in as many ways as there are people on this earth, and it comes through all forms of expression. It is connected to every person, every location, and every activity. As human beings, we are innately spiritual, and our spirituality can be expressed through recognizing what inspires us.

Our spirituality is a daily expression of what is most meaningful, most fulfilling, and holds the greatest purpose for us. We feel most fulfilled by the contribution we make to our own lives and the lives of others.

If you are happiest when you are focused on your business, then running your business is your form of spirituality. If what's most important to you is your children, then putting time into your family is your way of expressing your spirituality. If you love connecting with others, then socializing may be your spiritual pursuit. If you love to exercise and maintain a healthy body, that could be your form of spirituality.

During the time we are here, we have opportunities to experience, evolve, and grow. All our life experiences are just prompts to wake us up to the underlying order of the Universe and see the bigger picture of who we are and what we are meant to do in this world.

Spirituality comes in all forms of expression and is not about doing things that are spiritual, but about doing what inspires you.

DAILY MISSION: Remember that being spiritual is not about what you do or only about who or what you believe in. It is a matter of how you approach your life. Whatever it is that you can't wait to get up to do, know that this is your form of spirituality. Don't judge it or compare it to someone else's. Find ways to do more of it.

CHAPTER 8
The Superhero's Guiding Principles of Life

1. **Nothing happens *to* you; everything happens *for* you.**
Every experience in your life is designed for your growth and evolution.

2. **In every situation, there is always a bigger picture to consider.**
Every challenge in your life has hidden benefits that support you in every way.

3. **You are responsible for your own happiness.**
Your perception is in your mind and in your control.

4. **Your life has a purpose, and you are here for a reason.**
The closer you are to knowing your authentic Self, the more purposeful is your life.

5. **No matter what, you are perfect in every way.**
You are in the right life and the right body. Accept yourself as you are.

6. **Everything you are doing or not doing is serving a purpose.**
You are in the right place, doing the right thing.

7. **There really is no "right" or "wrong," only what's right for you.**
You have the right answers for you, even though others may say they know better.

8. **There are no "accidents" in your life.**
All synchronicities, wanted or unwanted, confirm that you are on the right path.

9. **Focus on your *own* life and your life will get easier.**
You can't make others do what you want them to do; let them live their life.

10. **Your own intuition is your best source of guidance.**
Ultimately no one knows better than you what is best for you.

OWN YOUR SUPERPOWERS

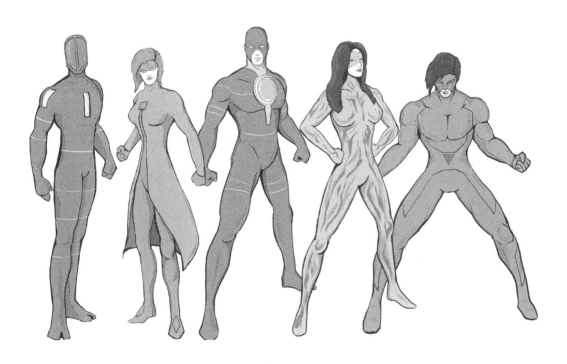

CHAPTER 9

THE UNIVERSAL ARCHENEMY

LESATH

DESCRIPTION: This villain archetype is treacherous to all superheroes and they share an infinite enmity with her. Lesath affects all archetypes and underhandedly weakens them, her goal being to keep them from living out their greatest power. Lesath emerged from the dark side and delights in making life's journey difficult. She will sabotage plans and betray trust at every turn. As the master of deceit, she exists in the outer tangible world of people and situations, as well as in the inner underworld of thoughts. She creates turmoil, perpetuates drama, spreads rumors, enhances worry, and ignites fears.

Gender	Female
Element	Polonium
Superpower	Deceit
Virtue	None
Other Superpowers	Negativity, Control, Fascination
Weaknesses	Love
Motto	"I win."
Core Desire	To come out on top
Core Value	To destroy
Life Goal	To take away the power of superheroes
Basic Fear	That attention will be taken away from her
Life Strategy	Looks for others' weaknesses and does everything to weaken them further
Personality Traits	Dishonest, Disloyal, Unethical, Suspicious, Hypocritical, Paranoid
Shape	Evasive
Power Colors	Purple
Power Number	0
Planet Affiliation	Pluto
Mythological Alliance	Medea
Animal affiliation	Scorpio

Lesath Is with You Forever

The story of our life is constructed out of a series of people and events. Every person we meet and every event that happens along the winding path of life transforms us from one state to another. Sometimes, these people and events support us and take us closer to our power, fulfillment, and happiness; other times, they take us farther away from our goals.

Situations, circumstances, and people frustrate us, betray us, and do everything they can to sabotage our success. The people we wish were not in our lives know our trigger points and seem to be there just to control us and drag us down. And, if it's not the people and the events that do it, it's that voice in our head that says we need to do more and be more, and that who we are is not enough.

Lesath is the archetype who comes from the dark and challenges us to dig deep within ourselves to find the light of our core power. She is also known as our ego— the self-consciousness system we all have that inhibits or legitimizes our identity and is the force that fuels all the negativities in our brain. The ego was founded in lack. It is what prevents you from being in touch with your essential and powerful wholeness.

Although we can never rid ourselves of Lesath's influence, the more light we nurture within ourselves, the less often she appears. However, the moment you feel uncertain or doubtful, she jumps into your head to agree with you, because that is where she thrives. At other times, she becomes the people who show up in your life.

During those intermittent times of challenge, we either give up, join the dark side, or grow to our next level of power. You are the hero in your life, and as you surpass the obstacles set by Lesath, you set yourself free. She helps you learn lessons about the world, about yourself, and most important, she helps you to rise to your greatest power.

About the Illustrator

In a cosmic sense, Jason Suapaia has been working on this project since he was ten years old—which is when he first began sketching superheroes on paper bags and using them for his textbook covers. These paper bags were canvases for his imagination, where the characters he created took flight. Characters like Batman inspired him to create an array of his own cast of original characters.

Illustration was such a powerful calling that Jason pursued a degree in commercial art and graphic design at Honolulu Community College. For more than twenty years, he has enjoyed an award-winning career in advertising, specializing in video and digital production. He currently serves as an executive for a prestigious international conglomerate that provides services in Hawaii.

Jason's Integrated Archetype, the Caring Perfectionist, has guided his pen, bringing to life Alice's collection of superheroes, an ethereal yet earth-bound cast that we all have within us.

About the Author

Award-wining author Alice Inoue is Hawaii's thought leader and celebrated expert on happiness and positivity. Throughout her career, she has helped tens of thousands of people find greater meaning and fulfillment.

Alice has published seven national award-winning books: *Be Happy! It's Your Choice; A Loving Guide to These Shifting Times; Feng Shui Your Life!; Just Ask Alice; Destination Happiness; Mindful Moments;* and *More Mindful Moments.* All focus on life wisdom, self-growth, and happiness.

Alice writes weekly columns for Hawaii's two largest publications, and is also the founder of Happiness U, a school in Honolulu devoted to personal growth and transformation.

Alice's Integrated Archetype, the Intuitive Luminary, has led her to inspire others and help them find their personal power. For more about Alice, visit **aliceinoue.com** and **yourhappinessu.com.**

Made in the USA
Las Vegas, NV
04 May 2023

71539689R00155